See you in Spring!
Love you.
Gerry
XXX.

MANCHESTER AUGUST 16. 1819.

SHELLEY'S REVOLUTIONARY YEAR

SHELLEY'S **REVOLUTIONARY** YEAR

Shelley's political poems and the essay *A Philosophical View of Reform*, with an introduction by Paul Foot

Shelley's Revolutionary Year
First Published April 1990
R E D **W** O R D S, 265 Seven Sisters Road
London N4 2DE
Introduction copyright © Paul Foot

ISBN 1 872208 00 2

Design by Roger Huddle
Typeset by Accent on Type, London EC1
Printed by Cox and Wyman Limited, Reading, England

Contents

Percy Bysshe Shelley was born in England in 1792, and was drowned in the Bay of Spezia, when his boat capsized in a storm, in 1822. He has been hailed as one of England's greatest poets—yet most of what is published here remained suppressed for a century after his death.

Paul Foot is author of the biography *Red Shelley* (London 1980), and a journalist. He is a member of the Socialist Workers Party. This book is published as a result of the enthusiasm of members of the SWP for Shelley's revolutionary writings.

INTRODUCTION

This is the first edition of a book which was proposed for publication 170 years ago by one of England's most famous writers. In May 1820 the poet Percy Bysse Shelley, who was living at Pisa in Italy, wrote two letters to his friend Leigh Hunt, publisher of the **Examiner**, a British radical monthly.

'I wish to ask you,' Shelley wrote in his first letter, 'if you know of any bookseller who would like to publish a little volume of popular songs wholly political, and destined to awaken and direct the imagination of the reformers. I see you smile—but answer my question.'

As part of the same package, he wrote in his second letter:

'One thing I want to ask you—do you know any bookseller who would publish for me an octavo volume entitled *A Philosophical View of Reform?* It is boldly, but temperately written, and I think readable. It is intended for a kind of standard book for the philosophical reformers politically considered, like Jeremy Bentham's something, but different and perhaps more systematic. I will send it sheet by sheet. Will you ask and think for me?'

Leigh Hunt never replied to either letter. Shelley chided his friend for never talking politics, and for never even responding to any request to publish his political writings. Leigh Hunt did not want to lose Shelley's friendship—he liked and admired the poet all his life—but he understood the laws on publishing in Britain in 1820.

He also knew how extreme were his friend's political views. He calculated, no doubt correctly, that any one of Shelley's 'popular songs', and any line of the *Philosophical View of Reform* would be instantly prosecuted, either under the vast array of laws which the Tory government of the time had passed in order to suppress 'sedition' or 'criminal libel' (both of which were then, as they are now, synonyms for criticism of the government), or through a private prosecution by the Society for the Prosecution of Vice, which was run by the Mary Whitehouses of the time. Shelley had never met the contemporary publishers, most notably Richard Carlile, who would have published his political work, especially if it entailed prosecution. He knew no one to turn to except Hunt, and Hunt was not amenable.

Thus the collection was not published in 1820—or at any other time since.

If Hunt had responded, there were certainly eight and possibly ten poems which Shelley would have sent for publication in *Popular Songs*. Together with the 15,000-word *Philosophical View of Reform*, they were all written in three and a half months at the end of 1819. This was perhaps the most sustained and prolific period of fine writing in British literary history. For Shelley wrote not just the ten poems and the 'octavo volume', but also his *Letter on Richard Carlile*, one of the greatest essays in support of free speech ever written in our language; *Peter Bell the Third*, a long satirical poem on the apostasy of Wordsworth; and a substantial slice of his most famous (and most difficult) poem *Prometheus Unbound*.

All this was inspired by a political event in Britain. In August 1819 a huge peaceful protest demonstration organised by the emerging trade unions met in carnival atmosphere at St Peter's Fields in Manchester. Before the speakers could properly address the meeting, it was attacked by the yeomanry, the special constabulary drawn from men of property. The gallant mounted burghers hacked their way through the unarmed crowd, killing eleven people with their swords and injuring many others. The British ruling class swaggered for months afterwards at the bravery of its 'stout yeomanry' at Peterloo—as the field of slaughter came to be known. Among the dispossessed and the new trade unionists there was a sullen but impotent fury.

Shelley heard the news of Peterloo on 5 September 1819, when he was living in Leghorn in Italy. He immediately sat down to write one of the great political protest poems of all time. *The Mask of Anarchy* starts with a furious attack on the Conservative administration in Britain. It recounts a nightmare in which the three Lords of the Tory Cabinet—Eldon the Lord Chancellor, Sidmouth the Home Secretary and above all Castlereagh, the Foreign Secretary— parade in an awful procession, murdering, deceiving and wheedling, while Britain dissolves into anarchy. The word 'anarchy' then meant something quite different to its normal meaning today. Shelley used it to describe the chaos of tyranny, in which no one but the very few who own and control society can plan their lives for themselves. Anarchy was 'God and King and Law', and its enemies were the common people of England. It 'slashed and stabbed' its way through the country, cutting down anyone who opposed the government.

Anarchy is itself destroyed in Shelley's poem by a 'maniac maid' who calls herself Hope, though she 'looked more like Despair'. She rouses the people to free themselves from their oppressors, by supplying them, among other things, with a powerful definition of freedom:

Thou art clothes and fire and food
For the trampled multitude.
No, in countries that are free
Such starvation cannot be
As in England now we see.

The speech of the 'maniac maid' identifies the central scandal in British society during the Industrial Revolution, the exploitation of the mass of workers by the new capitalists. That exploitation will continue, she warns—indeed there is no depth to which it will not sink—unless the masses do something about it. The central theme and message of this magnificent poem is agitation. What should be agitated for is a question which the poem does not always answer. Shelley himself seems to have been unclear about it. He appeals for a great demonstration which will engage in mass civil disobedience and thus shame the rulers into doing something about the oppressed. This mild, if unlikely, proposition, however, is contradicted by the famous last verse of the poem which calls on the 'many' to 'rise like lions' against the few and 'shake your chains to earth'. For much of the poem Shelley seems to be counselling the people to behave constitutionally, and to protest within the system. At other times, however, and especially at the end of the poem, he seems to be openly advocating revolution.

These themes, and this contradiction, run through the other poems in the collection.

Three of these are further expressions of fury against the Tory government: *Lines written during the Castlereagh Administration*, the *Sonnet: England 1819*, and the *Similes for Two Political Characters*. These poems are almost frenzied in their passionate hatred for the Crown and its ministers,

> ... who neither see nor feel nor know
> But leech-like to their fainting country cling.

The *Similes for Two Political Characters*—they are Castlereagh and Sidmouth—literally hiss and spit with Shelley's contempt for the two ministers.

Three other poems concentrate on the theme of exploitation. Shelley was shocked by poverty; but even more shocked by the contrast between poverty and riches. The song *Men of England* asks the people why they work for those who pay them next to nothing and then use the produce of their labour to oppress them. This poem ends with an appeal which comes surprisingly from a constitutionalist:

> Forge arms in your defence to bear.

In the *Ballad of the Starving Mother*, Shelley singles out the church for special attack. He never lost his admiration for Jesus

Christ, but was outraged by the way in which comfortable and contented churchmen sang the praises of Jesus while behaving in a manner which would have sent Jesus into tantrums of fury. *The Ballad* is often held out by critics of Shelley as an example of banal and stunted poetry into which, they allege, Shelley always degenerated when he turned his mind to politics and social conditions. It is true that the poem has none of the high flights of fancy nor the lyrical splendour which enrich so much of Shelley's poetry. But it is also obvious that this is deliberate: that the pace and tone of the ballad are dictated by the shocking story it tells. At times the starkness of the language is almost ridiculous, but the hatred which Shelley harboured for wealthy rural fops who grew fat by practising religion, while turning their backs on the growing ranks of the poor in their own congregations, forced him, often to excess, to abandon what Thomas Paine once called 'the ornaments' of language, and tell his story in monosyllables.

The tiny fragment *What Men Gain Fairly* was an attempt by Shelley to rationalise his views about private property. It amounts to little more than the platitude that people are entitled to what they can make for themselves by honest endeavour. The problem with this is the question it immediately provokes: what is honest endeavour, and what *isn't*? Shelley's poem makes an attempt to draw a line between the two, chiefly by examples. He cannot, however, wriggle out of the subjectivity of the test he applies. One man will claim honest endeavour where another man will claim, to use Shelley's words, that it is 'fraud and force'.

To some extent Shelley's uncertainty on this point was attributable to the time in which he lived. His short adult life (he was born in 1792, and was drowned in the Gulf of Spezia, when his boat capsized in a storm, in 1822—he was only 29) spanned the most cataclysmic period of the industrial revolution. Shelley saw and detested the new exploitation which was being ushered in by industrial capitalism. But he could not distinguish, as socialists later did, between owning the means of production, and owning *possessions* which flowed from that production.

The source of exploitation was the ownership and control of the means of production—whether the land or the new machinery and factories—by a tiny minority. If those means of production were democratically owned, controlled and planned, the source of exploitation would quickly dry up. Enemies of egalitarianism, in Shelley's time as now, argued that equality meant austerity, philistinism and sameness. On the contrary, however, once the means of production were controlled and owned by society, there would be no limit to the distribution of what flowed from that production; nor in the variety of human intelligences and passions which could be inspired by such distribution. The new age was not one of scarcity but of plenty.

A New National Anthem was a skit on Royal and Revered words, and was intensely seditious. It proposed a new Queen of England to be praised instead of the 'old mad blind despised and dying King', George the Third. The new Queen was Liberty.

It was this poem which would probably have persuaded Shelley to include in his little collection two more poems which later became famous. The first was the *Ode to Liberty*, which is prefaced with Byron's assertion that the banner of Freedom is always flying *against* the wind. Byron admired Shelley above all else for his constant struggling against the political current. Shelley's enormous talents were used not to butter up the rulers of society (as Wordsworth, Southey and Coleridge did) but to attack those rulers from every vantage point.

The *Ode to Liberty*, and the *Ode to the West Wind* which was to conclude the collection, were written in the high-flown lyrical style normally associated with Shelley. Both poems draw deeply not only on his lyrical talent but also on his vast intellect. But both were written in the same period as the shorter, angrier poems, and both come from the same stable. There are passages, especially in the *Ode to Liberty*, when Shelley turns directly on the kings and priests whom he detested, where the language becomes even more violent than it does in the shorter poems.

But the distinguishing feature of the *Ode to Liberty* for this collection is its vision of a new society. Shelley was not, as many idealists and egalitarians were then and are today, an empty idealist looking back to days in the past when men and women treated each other decently and revelled equally in a pastoral communism. There probably never were any days like that anyway, and the people who celebrated them—most of whom can be found today in the Green Party—have about them that smug hypocrisy which caused George Orwell to denounce them as 'bananas and sandals socialists'. Shelley sometimes slipped into romantic reveries about 'the old laws of England' which he imagined upheld the idea of freedom, but mostly he was fascinated by the new wonders of science and technology as potential instruments of an egalitarian and just society. He did not want to go back to dancing around the maypole. He wanted to go forward to a new world where the inventions and marvels of science could be put to their proper use: alleviating the condition of mankind and creating a New World of Plenty.

What if earth can clothe and feed
Amplest millions at their need,
And power in thought be as the tree within the seed?

The publication of these ten poems, however, would have been fruitless unless they were accompanied, either in the same volume or in a simultaneous one, by a long essay in which Shelley set out his political ideas. He wrote the *Philosophical View of Reform* in a notebook. He altered quite a lot of it, and obviously worked hard on it until the deafening silence from Hunt obliged him to abandon it. The first and most miserable result of this is that the pamphlet was never finished. It comes down to us still in rough draft, curiously (for Shelley) unpolished and at times even uncertain of its language. But it remains an extraordinary piece of work, and was described by Kenneth Neill Cameron, one of the most distinguished of all Shelley scholars, as 'the most advanced work of political theory of the age'.

The pamphlet starts with a broad sweep of the history of the peoples of the world up to 1819. History, Shelley insists, is not a series of events which happen accidentally, to be learnt by rote by reluctant school pupils. There is a thread to it: the remorseless battle between those at the top of society and the people in revolt against them. At one stage (where the text is, infuriatingly, unfinished) Shelley comes close to saying that the history of all hitherto existing society is the history of class struggle:

> Regular and alternate systems of alternate slavery and tyranny, by which all except the lowest and the largest class were to be the gainers in the materials of subsistence and ostentation at the expense of that class, the means being fraud and force, were established in the shape of feudal monarchies.

In this early and exhilarating section, Shelley notices that periodic outbursts in artistic and literary creation correspond to popular and social movements. As people rise against their oppressors so, as in the period in which Shelley lived, all kinds of talents and abilities are suddenly and simultaneously discovered.

Revolutions are the hinges of history, Shelley concludes. He compares in political and economic terms the English Revolution of the seventeenth century and the French Revolution of his own time. He supports the execution of the English King in 1649 and, by implication, he supports the execution of the French King in the year after Shelley himself was born (1793). He condemns the counter-revolution in both countries. He dwells at some length on the social and political developments in Britain in the hundred years between the counter-revolution of 1688 and the French Revolution, and notices in particular the emergence of two new classes in society. The first were the 'capitalists', whom he attacks with the most ferocious savagery; the second the 'unrepresented multitude', who were populating huge cities where there had previously been nothing but villages. In the process, this 'new class' was making a mockery of the system of 'pocket borough' representation in an entirely unrepresentative and reactionary House of Commons.

Shelley set out to write a 'temperate' pamphlet, to curb his own revolutionary passions and to settle for relatively minor reforms as a start in the process of reform. He finds this understandably difficult, and the pamphlet is marked throughout with contradictions. He holds off from calling for immediate and total adult suffrage but argues instead for an extension of the vote to people 'of small property'. Almost immediately, however, he proposes a scheme for a popular and representative parliament which in effect *is* elected on universal suffrage. He holds off calling for women's suffrage, but then at once apologises, explaining that he himself is very much in favour of it. When he comes to his basic demands, he is vague about the vote, though he insists on 'some form of government' able to carry out reforms. The demands he does make, however, are strong ones: abolition of the national debt, disbandment of the standing army, abolition of all sinecures, disestablishment of religion and the abolition of tithes, and justice which is cheap, and preferably only by jury.

Again and again the pamphlet is dogged by the same problem which dogs *The Mask of Anarchy*. What happens when, as seems likely, the rulers refuse to accede to such demands, do not extend the franchise, do not let up on their exploitation of the people, redouble their taxes, tithes, priests, judges and spies? Shelley's pamphlet moves from one compromise to the next, holding out for the absolute minimum of reform necessary to shift society even a little in the direction of progress. Continually, however, he is confronted by his own startling conclusion:

So dear is power that the tyrants themselves neither then, nor now, nor ever, left or leave a path to freedom but through their own blood.

'The last resort of resistance is undoubtedly insurrection,' he concludes, and forces himself to the probability that 'an appeal to an exertion of physical strength' will be necessary. Just as he is about to spell out the grim consequences of such a course of action, the pamphlet breaks off, leaving two blank pages which Shelley obviously planned to fill in later, perhaps when he had more closely worked out the complex relationship between reform and revolution. The final short peroration, which is weak enough as it is, appears, after this gap in the argument, even banal.

The uncertainties and doubts carry over into the economic sections of the pamphlet. These rely far too heavily on William Cobbett's theory that the blame for all British troubles could be placed on the national debt. It is true, as Shelley shows, that the national debt supplied Britain's ruling class with an excellent excuse to demand more regressive taxes from the poor or nearly poor. But the national debt was a symptom of the disease rather than its cause.

Nevertheless there is about the pamphlet a distinctly 'Marxist' tone, though this could hardly have come from Karl Marx, who was, when the *Philosophical View of Reform* was written, one year old. Shelley's analysis cuts society into two classes, the exploited and the exploiters. More subtle are those passages in the pamphlet which deal with the technological advances made by the industrial revolution and which, because of the way society was organised, were 'turned against themselves'. What could have been used to make every single person happy was instead used to conquer people in other countries, and further to rob the dispossessed. The idea is a prelude to Marx's much more sophisticated analysis of how the productive relations eventually become a 'fetter' on the productive forces, leading to all kinds of revolutionary consequences. Marx wrote all this *forty years* after Shelley had written his pamphlet.

Kenneth Cameron suggests that Shelley stands, in the radical tradition, 'about half way between Godwin and Marx'. William Godwin, Shelley's father-in-law, had written in the year of Shelley's birth a huge expensive book titled **Political Justice**, some of whose ideas formed part of Shelley's work. Godwin, however, was a middle-class reformer. He dealt only with the middle classes and cautioned his hot-headed son-in-law never to get involved in parties, associations, or indeed with any other people of similar persuasion.

Thomas Paine, on the other hand, whose book **The Rights of Man** was published in the same year as Godwin's **Political Justice**, was a man of action—a man who had taken part in and helped to inspire the American Revolution, and had tried to start a similar process in Britain. When he failed, and was driven into exile, Paine took his place in the Convention created by the French Revolution. **The Rights of Man** argued passionately for representative government, for the common people to take control of their destinies. Paine seldom dealt with the problem of property. One man, one vote, he thought, would lead automatically to a just and democratic society.

Shelley recognised much more than Paine that when property is unevenly distributed, when it is owned and controlled by a tiny minority, the purpose and thrust of universal suffrage can be vitiated. He was moving, not too clearly but persuasively, towards an understanding of property and economics which could recognise and describe the real divisions in the world. The *Philosophical View of Reform* was ready for its reluctant publisher in 1820, twenty-eight years after Paine's **The Rights of Man** and twenty-eight years before the **Communist Manifesto** by Karl Marx and Frederick Engels. In its ideas too, it falls half way between the two.

The *Philosophical View of Reform* stands squarely in the revolutionary tradition. There are of course indications that Shelley, with his high birth and inherited wealth, and in his (self-imposed) isolation from like-minded revolutionaries, yearned for the day when reform could come about by peaceful and constitutional means. But again and again he returns to the theme that when the die is cast, and when a choice has to be made between reform *by whatever means* and reaction, there is no alternative but to side with reform.

The best part of this pamphlet echoes the best parts of Shelley's political poetry. These are the passages which call on his fellow human beings to throw off their apathy. Shelley detested acceptance, obedience and passivity. He wanted challenge: challenge in argument and if necessary challenge in the streets. In a glorious passage towards the end of the pamphlet, Shelley calls on people *not to wait*, not to 'wait until those neutral politicians whose opinions represent the actions of their class are persuaded that some effectual reform is necessary'. The main enemy, he argues, is quietism, which allows people to sink into supineness. In this regard Shelley even opposed the secret ballot, on the grounds that people should be seen and heard to say and vote for what they believe, and that the 'republican boldness of censuring and judging one another' should be encouraged. It is this accent on agitation, as in his poems, which makes the reading of this pamphlet so exhilarating.

Margaret Thatcher, British prime minister in the 1980s, has on more than one occasion likened her administration to that of Lord Liverpool from 1812 to 1822. There are plenty of characteristics which Mrs Thatcher's Britain holds in common with Lord Liverpool's Britain. There is the same exploitation, the same patronising snobbery, the same blind belief in the military, the same lust for wars, the same suppression of opposition views. The language and passion of Shelley in 1819 is a wonderful inspiration to anyone who feels the same about Mrs Thatcher as Shelley felt about Lords Liverpool, Castlereagh, Sidmouth and Eldon. There are plenty of passages here which seem to have been written for the present time. While discussing the declining influence of the monarchy, for instance, Shelley writes in the *Philosophical View of Reform*: 'Monarchy is only the string which ties the robber's bundle.' That sentence made a good headline for **Socialist Worker**'s coverage of the Royal Jubilee of Queen Elizabeth in 1977.

What happened, then, to these poems and the pamphlet which were submitted by Shelley to Leigh Hunt for publication in 1820? Only two of them—the *Ode to Liberty* and the *Ode to the West Wind*—were published in Shelley's lifetime, in 1820. Hunt did, eventually, publish three others. *The Mask of Anarchy*, the *Lines written during the Castlereagh Administration* and the *Similes for Two Political Characters* were published in 1832, ten years after Shelley's death, to coincide with the agitation around the new Reform Bill. In 1839, the year of the first Chartist uprising, which is probably the closest Britain ever came to a working-class revolution, Mary Shelley published the *Song to the Men of England*, *What Men Gain Fairly* and *The New National Anthem*. *The Ballad of the Starving*

Mother, which was considered such bad poetry by Shelley-worshippers, did not get published until 1926, and then only in a collection. It was not published as a single poem until 1970, a hundred and fifty years after it was written.

The *Philosophical View of Reform* was not published at all in the hundred years after it was written. Shelley's notebook was passed from hand to hand until 1920, when T W Rolleston published it as a special edition for members of the Shelley Society. Perhaps 500 copies were printed and circulated. Probably none at all can be found in even the most sophisticated second-hand booksellers today.

It is right and proper that a socialist publisher should fulfil the wishes of a great revolutionary poet 170 years ago. For the ideas which Shelley expressed, and which no one outside his circle listened to during his lifetime, are ideas which carry easily and freely through the ages.

Above all else, he calls on people who understand the way society is corrupted, and who believe that by their actions people can change that society and end that corruption, to stay loyal to the principles of their youth, and not bend under the blandishments or threats of their rulers. In his greatest poem, the *Ode to the West Wind*, which he wrote in October 1819 after reading a vitriolic attack on him in an English journal, he conjured up the dilemma of any revolutionary who, once the 'first fine careless rapture' of the revolutionary idea has been absorbed, is plagued with loneliness and disillusionment. The gradual realisation that not everyone agrees; that in spite of the obvious necessity for revolutionary change it has not come about; that we (who may be many) are weak, while they (the few) are strong; these lead countless revolutionaries into compromise, collaboration, cynicism and despair. Shelley's language, especially in these poems and this essay, catches hold of the falling revolutionary and puts him or her back on their feet.

Shelley himself was raddled with doubt. *The Ode to the West Wind* is a poem about his doubt. The revolution was not all daffodils and daisies as Wordsworth and thousands of others had thought.

The revolution held out the prospect of 'living hues and odours', but often produced nothing but 'black rain, and hail and fire'. For revolutionaries as they grow older, everything suddenly seems more difficult, more unlikely. Children race across the meadows to try to beat the clouds which scud across the sky. They fail, but they try again. And again, perhaps. But when the clouds always win, they tend to give up.

That was how Shelley felt, in October 1819, insulted by the literary and cultural world, shunned by almost all writers of merit, his children dead in infancy or taken from him because he was an atheist, his work seldom published for fear of prosecution. But in the last verse of his greatest poem he calls on the revolutionary wind to dispel his doubts, his uncertainties, his domestic difficulties, and to shape and carry his revolutionary message to 'unawakened earth' so that the winter of Tory corruption can change into the revolutionary spring.

Socialists should not seek to persuade their children by dunning them with dogmatic propaganda. But socialists have a duty to their children to bribe or bully them to learn the poetry which carries revolutionary ideas through the centuries, in the minds of those who remember and sense it. Here is a marvellous, cheap volume from which no individual will make a single penny (as Shelley didn't). Start with *The Mask of Anarchy* and work your way through to the last verse of the *Ode to the West Wind*. Reinforce it all with the irresistible message of the *Philosophical View of Reform*. And rise like lions.

Paul Foot, 21 May 1989.

A PHILOSOPHICAL VIEW OF REFORM

FOREWORD

Those who imagine that their personal interest is directly or indirectly concerned in maintaining the power in which they are clothed by the existing institutions of English Government do not acknowledge the necessity of a material change in those institutions ... With this exception, there is no inhabitant of the British Empire of mature age and perfect understanding not fully persuaded of the necessity of Reform. Let us believe not only that [it] is necessary because it is just and ought to be, but necessary because it is inevitable and must be.

OUTLINE

1st. Sentiment of the necessity of change.
2nd. Practicability and utility of such a change.
3rd. State of parties as regards it.
4th. Probable mode—desirable mode.

Chapter 1

INTRODUCTION

From the dissolution of the Roman Empire, that vast and successful scheme for the enslaving [of] the most civilised portion of mankind, to the epoch of the present year have succeeded a series of schemes on a smaller scale, operating to the same effect. Names borrowed from the life and opinions of Jesus Christ were employed as symbols of domination and imposture, and a system of liberty and equality (for such was the system preached by that great Reformer) was perverted to support oppression—not his doctrines, for they are too simple and direct to be susceptible of such perversion, but the mere names. Such was the origin of the Catholic Church, which, together with the several dynasties then beginning to consolidate themselves in Europe, means, being interpreted, a plan according to which the cunning and selfish few have employed the fears and hopes of the ignorant many to the establishment of their own power and the destruction of the real interest of all.

The republics and municipal governments of Italy opposed for some time a systematic and effectual resistance to the all-surrounding tyranny. The Lombard League defeated the armies of the despot in open field, and until Florence was betrayed to those flattered traitors [and] polished tyrants, the Medici, Freedom had one citadel wherein it could find refuge from a world which was its enemy. Florence long balanced, divided, and weakened the strength of the Empire and the Popedom. To this cause, if to anything, was due the undisputed superiority of Italy in literature and the arts over all its contemporary nations, that union of energy and of beauty which distinguish[es] from all other poets the writings of Dante, that restlessness of fervid power which expressed itself in painting and sculpture and in daring architectural forms, and from which, and conjointly from the creations of Athens, its predecessor and its image, Raphael and Michel Angelo drew the inspiration which created those forms and colours now the astonishment of the world. The father of our own literature, Chaucer, wrought from the simple and powerful language of a nursling of this republic the basis of our own literature. And thus we owe among other causes the exact condition belonging to [our own] intellectual existence to the generous disdain of submission which burned in the bosoms of men who filled a distant generation and inhabited another land.

When this resistance was overpowered (as what resistance to fraud and [tyranny] has not been overpowered?) another was even then maturing. The progress of philosophy and civilisation which ended in that imperfect emancipation of mankind from the yoke of priests and kings called the Reformation had already commenced. Exasperated by their long sufferings, inflamed by the spark of that superstition from the flames of which they were emerging, the poor rose against their natural enemies, the rich, and repaid with bloody interest the tyranny of ages. One of the signs of the times was that the oppressed peasantry rose like the negro slaves of West Indian plantations and murdered their tyrants when they were unaware. For so dear is power that the tyrants themselves neither then, nor now, nor ever, left or leave a path to freedom but through their own blood. The contest then waged under the names of religion—which have seldom been any more [than] the popular and visible symbols which express the degree of power in some shape or other asserted by one party and disclaimed by the other—ended; and the result, though partial and imperfect, is perhaps the most animating that the philanthropist can contemplate in the history of man. The Republic of Holland, which has been so long an armoury of arrows of learning by which superstition has been wounded even to death, was established by this contest. What though the name of Republic—and by whom but by conscience-stricken tyrants could it be extinguished—is no more? The Republics of Switzerland derived from this event their consolidation and their union. From England then first began to pass away the strain of conquest. The exposition of a certain portion of religious imposture drew with it an inquiry into political imposture and was attended with an extraordinary exertion of the energies of intellectual power. Shakespeare and Lord Bacon and the great writers of the age of Elizabeth and James I were at once the effects of the new spirit in men's minds and the causes of its more complete development. By rapid gradation the nation was conducted to the temporary abolition of aristocracy and episcopacy, and [to] the mighty example which, 'in teaching nations how to live,' England afforded to the world—of bringing to public justice one of those chiefs of a conspiracy of privileged murderers and robbers whose impunity has been the consecration of crime [the execution of Charles I].

After the selfish passions and compromising interests of men had enlisted themselves to produce and establish the restoration of Charles II the unequal combat was renewed under the reign of his successor [James II], and that compromise between the inextinguishable spirit of Liberty and the ever-watchful spirit of fraud and tyranny, called the Revolution [of 1688], had place. On this occasion monarchy and aristocracy and episcopacy were at once established and limited by law. Unfortunately they lost no more in extent of power than they gained in security of possession. Meanwhile those by whom they were established acknowledged and declared that the will of the people was the source from which these powers, in this instance, derived the right to subsist. A man has no right to be a king or lord or a bishop but so long as it is for the benefit of the people and so long as the people judge that it is for their benefit that he should impersonate that character. The solemn establishment of this maxim as the basis of our constitutional law more than any beneficial and energetic application of it to the circumstances of this era of its promulgation was the fruit of that vaunted event. Correlative with this series of events in England was the commencement of a new epoch in the history of the progress of civilisation and society.

That superstition which had disguised itself under the name of the religion of Jesus subsisted under all its forms, even where it had been separated from those things especially considered as abuses by the multitude, in the shape of intolerant and oppressive hierarchies. Catholics massacred Protestants and Protestants proscribed Catholics, and extermination was the sanction of each faith within the limits of the power of its professors. The New Testament is in everyone's hand, and the few who ever read it with the simple sincerity of an unbiased judgement may perceive how distinct from the opinions of any of those professing themselves establishers [of churches] were the doctrines and the actions of Jesus Christ. At the period of the Reformation this test was applied, and this judgement formed of the then existing hierarchy, and the same compromise was then made between the spirit of truth and the spirit of imposture after [the] struggle which ploughed up the area of the human mind as was made in the particular instance of England between the spirit of freedom and the spirit of tyranny at that event called the Revolution [of 1688]. In both instances the maxims so solemnly recorded remain as trophies of our difficult and incomplete victory, planted in the enemies' land. *The will of the people to change their government is an acknowledged right in the Constitution of England*. The protesting against religious dogmas which present themselves to his mind as false is the inalienable prerogative of every human being.

The new epoch was marked by the commencement of deeper inquiries into the forms of human nature than are compatible with an unreserved belief in any of those popular mistakes upon which popular systems of faith with respect to the cause and agencies of the universe, with all their superstructure of political and religious tyranny, are built. Lord Bacon, Spinoza, Hobbes, Bayle, Montaigne regulated the reasoning powers, criticised the past history, exposed the errors by illustrating their causes and their connection, and anatomised the inmost nature of social man. Then, with a less interval of time than of genius followed [Locke] and the philosophers of his exact and intelligible but superficial school. Their illustrations of some of the minor consequences of the doctrines established by the sublime genius of their predecessors were correct, popular, simple, and energetic. Above all, they indicated inferences the most incompatible with the popular religions and the established governments of Europe. [Philosophy went forth into the enchanted forest of the demons of worldly power as the pioneer of the over-growth of ages.] Berkeley, and Hume, [and] Hartley [at a] later age, following the traces of these inductions, have clearly established the certainty of our ignorance with respect to those obscure questions which under the name of religious truths have been the watch-words of contention and the symbols of unjust power ever since they were distorted by the narrow passions of the immediate followers of Jesus from that meaning to which philosophers are even now restoring them. A crowd of writers in France seized upon the most popular portions of the new philosophy which conducted to inferences at war with the dreadful oppressions under which the country groaned made familiar to mankind the falsehood of their religious mediators and political oppressors. Considered as philosophers their error seems to have consisted chiefly of a limitedness of view; they told the truth, but not the whole truth. This might have arisen from the terrible sufferings of their countrymen inviting them rather to apply a portion of what had already been discovered to their immediate relief than to pursue one interest, the abstractions of thought, as the great philosophers who preceded them had done, for the sake of a future and more universal advantage. While that philosophy which, burying itself in the obscure part of our nature, regards the truth and falsehood of dogmas relating to the cause of the universe and the nature and manner of man's relation with it, was thus stripping power of its darkest mask, political philosophy, or that which considers the relations of man as a social being, was assuming a precise form. This philosophy indeed sprang from and maintained a connection with that other as its parent. What would Swift and Bolingbroke and Sidney [Algernon] and Locke and Montesquieu, or even Rousseau, not to speak of political philosophers of our own age, Godwin and Bentham, have been but for Lord Bacon, Montaigne, and Spinoza, and other great luminaries of the preceding epoch? Something excellent and eminent, no doubt, the least of these would have been, but something different from and inferior to what they are. A series of these writers illustrated with more or less success the principles of human nature as applied to man in political society. A thirst for accommodating the existing forms according to which mankind are found divided to those rules of freedom and equality which are thus discovered as being the elementary principles according to which the happiness resulting from the social union ought to be produced and distributed was kindled by these inquiries. Contemporary with this condition of the intellect all the powers of man seemed, though in most cases under forms highly inauspicious, to develop themselves with uncommon energy. The mechanical sciences attained to a degree of perfection which, though obscurely foreseen by Lord Bacon, it had been accounted madness to have prophesied in a preceding age. Commerce was pursued with a perpetually increasing vigour, and the same area of the earth was perpetually compelled to furnish more and more subsistence. The means and sources of knowledge were thus increased together with knowledge itself and the instruments of knowledge. The benefit of this increase of the powers of man became, in consequence of the inartificial forms into which society came to be distributed, an instrument of his additional evil. The capabilities of happiness were increased and applied to the augmentation of misery. Modern society is thus an engine assumed to be for useful purposes, whose force is by a system of subtle mechanism augmented to the highest pitch, but which, instead of grinding corn or raising water, acts against itself and is perpetually wearing away or breaking to pieces the wheels of which it is composed. The result of the labours of the political philosophers has been the establishment of the principle of utility as the substance and liberty and equality as the forms, according to which the concerns of human life ought to be administered. By this test the various institutions regulating political society have been tried and, as the undigested growth of the private passions, errors, and interests of barbarians and oppressors have been condemned. And many new theories, more or less perfect, but all superior to the mass of evil which they would supplant, have been given to the world.

The system of government in the United States of America was the first practical illustration of the new philosophy. Sufficiently remote, it will be confessed, from the accuracy of ideal excellence is that representative system which will soon cover the extent of that vast Continent. But it is scarcely less remote from the insolent and contaminating tyrannies under which, with some limitation of these terms as regards England, Europe groaned at the period of the successful rebellion of America. America holds forth the victorious example of an immensely populous and, as far as the external arts of life are concerned, a highly civilised community administered according to republican forms. It has no king; that is, it has no officer to whom wealth and from whom corruption flows. It has no hereditary oligarchy; that is, it acknowledges no order of men privileged to cheat and insult the rest of the members of the state and who inherit a right of legislating and judging which the principles of human nature compel them to exercise to their own profit and to the detriment of those not included within their peculiar class. It has no established church; that is, it has no system of opinions respecting the abstrusest questions which can be topics of human thought founded in an age of error and fanaticism and opposed by law to all other opinions, defended by prosecutions and sanctioned by enormous bounties given to idle priests and forced through the unwilling hands of those who have an interest in the cultivation and improvement of the soil. It has no false representation, whose consequences are captivity, confiscation, infamy, and ruin, but a true representation. The will of the many is represented by the few in the assemblies of legislation and by the officers of the executive entrusted with the administration of the executive power almost as directly as the will of one person can be represented by the will of another. [This is not the place for dilating upon the inexpressible advantages (if such advantages require any manifestation) of self-governing society, or one which approaches it in the degree of the Republic of the United States.] Lastly, it has an institution by which it is honourably distinguished from all other governments which ever existed. It constitutionally acknowledges the progress of human improvement and is framed under the limitation of the probability of more simple views of political science being rendered applicable to human life. There is a law by which the constitution is reserved for revision every ten years. [*Editor's note:* Such a clause was proposed but not adopted.] Every other set of men who have assumed the office of legislation and framing institutions for future ages, with far less right to such an assumption than the founders of the American Republic, assumed that their work was the wisest and the best that could possibly have been produced; these illustrious men [on the other hand] looked upon the past history of their species and saw that it was the history of his mistakes and his sufferings arising from his mistakes; they observed the superiority of their own work to all the works which had preceded it, and they judged it probable that other political institutions would be discovered bearing the same relation to those which they had established which they bear to those which have preceded them. They provided therefore for the application of these contingent discoveries to the social state without the violence and misery attendant upon such change in less modest and more imperfect governments. The United States, as we would have expected from theoretical deduction, affords an example, compared with the old governments of Europe and Asia, of a free, happy, and strong people. Nor let it be said that they owe their superiority rather to the situation than to their government. Give them a king, and let that king waste in luxury, riot, and bribery the same sum which now serves for the entire expenses of their government. Give them an aristocracy, and let that aristocracy legislate for the people. Give them a priesthood, and let them bribe with a tenth of the produce of the soil a certain set of men to say a certain set of words. Pledge the larger part of them by financial subterfuges to pay the half of their property or earnings to another portion, and let the proportion of those who enjoy the fruits of the toil of others without toiling themselves be three instead of one. Give them a Court of Chancery, and let the property, the liberty, and the interest in the dearest concerns of life, the exercise of the most sacred rights of a social being, depend upon the will of one of the most servile creature[s] of that kingly and oligarchical and priestly power to which every man in proportion as he is of an inquiring and philosophical mind and of a sincere and honourable disposition is a natural, a necessary enemy. Give them, as you must if you give them these things, a great standing army to cut down the people if they murmur. If any American should see these words, his blood would run cold at the imagination of such a change. He well knows that the prosperity and happiness of the United States if subjected to such institutions [would] be no more.

The just and successful revolt of America corresponded with a state of public opinion in Europe of which it was the first result. The French Revolution was the second. The oppressors of mankind had enjoyed (O that we could say suffered) a long and undisturbed reign in France, and to the pining famine, the shelterless destitution of the inhabitants of that country had been added and heaped-up insult harder to endure than misery. For the feudal system (the immediate causes and conditions of its institution having become obliterated) had degenerated into an instrument not only of oppression but of contumely, and both were unsparingly inflicted. Blind in the possession of strength, drunken as with the intoxication of ancestral greatness, the rulers perceived not that increase of knowledge in their subjects which made its exercise insecure. They called soldiers to hew down the people when their power was already past. The tyrants were, as usual, the aggressors. Then the oppressed, having being rendered brutal, ignorant, servile, and bloody by long slavery, having had the intellectual thirst excited in them by the progress of civilisation, satiated from fountains of literature poisoned by the spirit and the form of monarchy, arose and took a dreadful revenge upon their oppressors. Their desire to wreak revenge to this extent, in itself a mistake, a crime, a calamity, arose from the same source as their other miseries and errors and affords an additional proof of the necessity of that long-delayed change which it accompanied and disgraced. If a just and necessary revolution could have been accomplished with as little expense of happiness and order in a country governed by despotic as [in] one governed by free laws, equal liberty and justice would lose their chief recommendations and tyranny be divested of its most revolting attributes. Tyranny entrenches itself within the existing interests of the most refined citizens of a nation and says, 'If you dare trample upon these, be free.' Though this terrible condition shall not be evaded, the world is no longer in a temper to decline the challenge.

The French were what their literature is (excluding Montaigne and Rousseau, and some few leaders of the . . .) weak, superficial, vain, with little imagination, and with passions as well as judgements cleaving to the external form of things. Not that [they] are organically different from the inhabitants of the nations who have become . . . or rather not that their organical differences, whatever they may amount to, incapacitate them from arriving at the exercise of the highest powers to be attained by man. Their institutions made them what they were. Slavery and superstition, contumely and the tame endurance of contumely, and the habits engendered from generation to generation out of this transmitted inheritance of wrong, created this thing which has extinguished what has been called the likeness of God in man. The Revolution in France overthrew the hierarchy, the aristocracy, and the monarchy, and the whole of that peculiarly insolent and oppressive system on which they were based. But as it only partially extinguished those passions which are the spirit of these forms a reaction took place which has restored in a certain limited degree the old system—in a degree, indeed, exceedingly limited, and stript of all its ancient terrors. The hope of the monarchy of France, with his teeth drawn and his claws pared, was its maintaining the formal likeness of most imperfect and insecure dominion. The usurpation of Bonaparte, and then the Restoration of the Bourbons were the shapes in which this reaction clothed itself, and the heart of every lover of liberty was struck as with palsy by the succession of these events. But reversing the proverbial expression of Shakespeare, it may be the good which the Revolutionists did lives after them, their ills are interred with their bones. But the military project of government of the great tyrant having failed, and there being even no attempt—and, if there were any attempt, there being not the remotest possibility of re-establishing the enormous system of tyranny abolished by the Revolution—France is, as it were, regenerated. Its legislative assemblies are in a certain limited degree representations of the popular will, and the executive power is hemmed in by jealous laws. France occupies in this respect the same situation as was occupied by England at the restoration of Charles II. It has undergone a revolution (unlike in the violence and calamities which attended it, because unlike in the abuses which it was excited to put down) which may be paralleled with that in our own country which ended in the death of Charles I. The authors of both revolutions proposed a greater and more glorious object than the degraded passions of their countrymen permitted them to attain. But in both cases abuses were abolished which never since have dared to show their face.

There remains in the natural order of human things that the tyranny and perfidy of the reigns of Charles II and James II (for these were less the result of the disposition of particular men than the vices which would have been engendered in any but an extraordinary man by the natural necessities of their situation) perhaps under a milder form and within a shorter period should produce the institution of a government in France which may bear the same relation to the state of political knowledge existing at the present day, as the Revolution under William III bore to the state of political knowledge existing at that period.

Germany, which is among the great nations of Europe one of

the latest civilised with the exception of Russia, is rising with the fervour of a vigorous youth th the assertion of those rights for which it has that desire arising from knowledge, the surest pledge of victory. The deep passion and the bold and Aeschylean vigour of the imagery of their poetry; the enthusiasm, however distorted, of their religious sentiments; the flexibility and comprehensiveness of their language, which is a many-sided mirror of every changing thought; their severe, bold, and liberal spirit of criticism; their subtle and deep philosophy, however erroneous and illogical [in] mingling fervid intuitions into truth with obscure error (for the period of just distinction is yet to come), and their taste and power in the plastic arts, prove that they are a great people. And every great people either has been, or is, or will be free. The panic-stricken tyrants of that country promised to their subjects that their governments should be administered according to republican forms, they retaining merely the right of hereditary chief magistracy in their families. This promise, made in danger, the oppressors dream that they can break in security. And everything in consequence wears in Germany the aspect of rapidly maturing revolution.

In Spain and in the dependencies of Spain good and evil in the forms of despair and tyranny are struggling foot to foot. That great people have been delivered bound hand and foot to be trampled upon and insulted by a traitorous and sanguinary tyrant, a wretch who makes credible all that might have been doubted in the history of Nero, Christiern, Muley Ismael, or Ezzelin—the persons who have thus delivered them were that hypocritical knot of conspiring tyrants who proceeded upon the credit they gained by putting down the only tyrant among them who was not a hypocrite to undertake the administration of those *arrondissements* of consecrated injustice and violence which they deliver to those who the nearest resemble them under the name of the 'kingdoms of the earth.' This action signed a sentence of death, confiscation, exile, or captivity against every philosopher and patriot in Spain. The tyrant Ferdinand, he whose name is changed into a proverb of execration, found natural allies in all the priests and a few of the most dishonourable military chiefs of that devoted country. And the consequences of military despotism and the black, stagnant, venomous hatred which priests in common with eunuchs seek every opportunity to wreak upon the portion of mankind exempt from their own unmanly disqualifications is slavery. And what is slavery—in its mildest form hideous and, so long as one amiable or great attribute survives in its victims, rankling and intolerable, but in its darkest shape [as] it now exhibits itself in Spain it is the presence of all and more than all the evils for the sake of an exemption from which mankind submit to the mighty calamity of government. It is a system of insecurity of property, and of person, of prostration of conscience and understanding, of famine heaped upon the greater number, and contumely heaped upon all, defended by unspeakable tortures employed not merely as punishments but as precautions, by want, death, and captivity, and the application to political purposes of the execrated and enormous instruments of religious cruelty. Those men of understanding, integrity, and courage who rescued their country from one tyrant are exiled from it by his successor and his enemy and their legitimate king. Tyrants, however they may squabble among themselves, have common friends and foes. The taxes are levied at the point of the sword. Armed insurgents occupy all the defensible mountains of the country. The dungeons are peopled thickly, and persons of every sex and age have the fibres of their frame torn by subtle torments. Boiling water (such is an article in the last news from Spain) is poured upon the legs of a noble Spanish Lady newly delivered, slowly and cautiously, that she may confess what she knows of a conspiracy against the tyrant, and she dies, as constant as the slave Epicharis, imprecating curses upon her torturers and passionately calling upon her children. These events, in the present condition of the understanding and sentiment of mankind, are the rapidly passing shadows which forerun successful insurrection, the ominous comets of our republican poet [Milton] perplexing great monarchs with fear of change. Spain, having passed through an ordeal severe in proportion to the wrongs and errors which it is kindled to erase, must of necessity be renovated. [The country which] produced Calderon and Cervantes, what else did it but breathe through the tumult of the despotism and superstition which invested them, the prophecy of a glorious consummation?

The independents of South America are as it were already free. Great republics are about to consolidate themselves in a portion of the globe sufficiently vast and fertile to nourish more human beings than at present occupy, with the exception perhaps of China, the remainder of the inhabited earth. Some indefinite arrears of misery and blood remain to be paid to the Moloch of oppression. These, to the last drop and groan, it will implacably exact. But not the less are [they] inevitably enfranchised. The great monarchies of Asia cannot, let us confidently hope, remain unshaken by the earthquake which shatters to dust the 'mountainous strongholds' of the tyrants of the western world.

Revolutions in the political and religious state of the Indian peninsula seem to be accomplishing, and it cannot be doubted but the zeal of the missionaries of what is called the Christian faith will produce beneficial innovation there, even by the application of dogmas and forms of what is here an outworn incumbrance. The Indians have been enslaved and cramped in the most severe and paralysing forms which were ever devised by man; some of this new enthusiasm ought to be kindled among them to consume it and leave them free, and even if the doctrines of Jesus do not penetrate through the darkness of that which those who profess to be his followers call Christianity, there will yet be a number of social forms modelled upon those European feelings from which it has taken its colour substituted to those according to which they are at present cramped, and from which, when the time for complete emancipation shall arrive, their disengagement may be less difficult, and under which their progress to it may be the less imperceptibly slow. Many native Indians have acquired, it is said, a competent knowledge in the arts and philosophy of Europe, and Locke and Hume and Rousseau are familiarly talked about in Brahminical society. But the thing to be sought is that they should as they would if they were free attain to a system of arts and literature of their own. Of Persia we know little but that it has been the theatre of sanguinary contests for power, and that it is now at peace. The Persians appear to be from organisation a beautiful, refined, and impassioned people and would probably soon be infected by the contagion of good. The Jews, that wonderful people which has preserved so long the symbols of their union, may reassume their ancestral seats, and—the Turkish Empire is in its last stage of ruin, and it cannot be doubted but that the time is approaching when the deserts of Asia Minor and of Greece will be colonised by the overflowing population of countries less enslaved and debased, and that the climate and the scenery which was the birthplace of all that is wise and beautiful will not remain forever the spoil of wild beasts and unlettered Tartars. In Syria and Arabia the spirit of human intellect has roused a sect of people called Wahabees, who maintain the Unity of God, and the equality of man, and their enthusiasm must go on 'conquering and to conquer' even if it must be repressed in its present shape. Egypt having but a nominal dependence upon Constantinople is under the government of Ottoman Bey, a person of enlightened views who is introducing European literature and arts, and is thus beginning that change which Time, the great innovator, will accomplish in that degraded country; [and] by the same means its sublime enduring monuments may excite lofty emotions in the hearts of the posterity of those who now contemplate them without admiration.

Lastly, in the West Indian islands, first from the disinterested yet necessarily cautious measures of the English nation, and then from the infection of spirit of Liberty in France, the deepest stain upon civilised man is fading away. Two nations of free negroes are already established; one, in pernicious mockery of the usurpation over France, an empire, the other a republic—both animating yet terrific spectacles to those who inherit around them the degradation of slavery and the peril of dominion.

Such is a slight sketch of the general condition of the human race to which they have been conducted after the obliteration of the Greek republics by the successful external tyranny of Rome—its internal liberty having been first abolished—and by those miseries and superstitions consequent upon this event which compelled the human race to begin anew its difficult and obscure career of producing, according to the forms of society, the great portion of good.

Meanwhile England, the particular object for the sake of which these general considerations have been stated on the present occasion, has arrived like the nations which surround it at a crisis in its destiny. The literature of England, an energetic development of which has ever followed or preceded a great and free development of the national will, has arisen, as it were, from a new birth. In spite of that low-thoughted envy which would undervalue, through a fear of comparison with its own insignificance, the eminence of contemporary merit, it is *felt by the British* [that] ours is in intellectual achievements a memorable age, and we live among such philosophers and poets as surpass beyond comparison any who have appeared in our nation since its last struggle for liberty. For the most unfailing herald, or companion, or follower, of an universal employment of the sentiments of a nation to the production of beneficial change is poetry, meaning by poetry an intense and impassioned power of communicating intense and impassioned impressions respecting man and nature. The persons in whom this power takes its abode may often, as far as regards many portions of their nature, have little tendency [to] the spirit of good of which it is the minister. But although they may deny and abjure, they are yet compelled to serve that which is seated on the throne of own soul. And whatever systems they may [have] professed by support, they actually advance the interests of liberty. It is impossible to read the productions of our most celebrated writers, whatever may be their system relating to thought or expression, without being startled by the electric life which there is in their words. They measure the circumference or sound the depths of human nature with a comprehensive and all-penetrating spirit at which they are themselves perhaps most sincerely astonished, for it [is] less their own spirit than the spirit of their age. They are the priests of an unapprehended inspiration, the mirrors of gigantic shadows which futurity casts upon the present; the words which express what they conceive not; the trumpet which sings to battle and feels not what it inspires; the influence which is moved not, but moves. Poets and philosophers are the unacknowledged legislators of the world.

But, omitting these more abstracted considerations, has there not been and is there not in England a desire of change arising from the profound sentiment of the exceeding inefficiency of the existing institutions to provide for the physical and intellectual happiness of the people? It is proposed in this work (1) to state and examine the present condition of this desire, (2) to elucidate its causes and its object, (3) to then show the practicability and utility, nay the necessity of change, (4) to examine the state of parties as regards it, and (5) to state the probable, the possible, and the desirable mode in which it should be accomplished.

Chapter 2

ON THE SENTIMENT OF THE NECESSITY OF CHANGE

Two circumstances arrest the attention of those who turn their regard to the present political condition of the English nation—first, that there is an almost universal sentiment of the approach of some change to be wrought in the institutions of the government, and secondly, the necessity and desirableness of such a change. From the first of these propositions, it being matter of fact, no person addressing the public can dissent. The latter, from a general belief in which the former flows and on which it depends, is matter of opinion, but [one] which to the mind of all, excepting those interested in maintaining the contrary is a doctrine so clearly established that even they, admitting that great abuses exist, are compelled to impugn it by insisting upon the specious topic, that popular violence, by which they alone could be remedied, would be more injurious than the continuance of these abuses. But as those who argue thus derive for the most part great advantage and convenience from the continuance of these abuses, their estimation of the mischiefs of uprising [and] popular violence as compared with the mischiefs of tyrannical and fraudulent forms of government are likely, from the known principles of human nature . . .

[*The following passage is omitted in Mary Shelley's transcription:* According to the principles of human nature as modified by the existing opinions and institutions of society a man loves himself with an overweaning love. The generous emotions of disinterested affection which the records of human nature and our experience teach us that the human heart is highly susceptible of are confined within the narrow circle of our kindred and friends. And therefore there is a class of men considerable from talents, influence, and station who of necessity are enemies to Reform.

For Reform would benefit the nation at their expense instead of suffering them to benefit themselves at the expense of the nation. If a reform however mild were to take place, they must submit to a diminution of those luxuries and vanities in the idolatry of which they have been trained. Not only they, but what in most cases would be esteemed a harder necessity their wives and children and dependents must be comprehended in the same restrictions. That degree of pain which however it is to be regretted is necessarily attached to the relinquishment of the habits of particular persons at war with the general permanent advantage, must be inflicted by the mildest reform. It is not alleged that every person whose interest is directly or indirectly concerned in the maintaining things as they are, is therefore necessarily interested. There are individuals who can be just judges even against themselves, and by study and self-examination have established a severe tribunal within themselves to which these principles which demand the advantages of the greater number are admitted to appeal. With some it assumes the mark of fear, with others that of hope—with all it is expectation.]

... to be exaggerated. Such an estimate comes too with a worse grace from them who, if they would in opposition to their own unjust advantage take the lead in reform, might spare the nation from the inconveniences of the temporary dominion of the poor who by means of that degraded condition which their insurrection would be designed to ameliorate are sufficiently incapable of discerning their own genuine and permanent advantage, though surely less incapable than those whose interests consist in proposing to themselves an object perfectly opposite [to] and wholly incompatible with that advantage: all public functionaries who are overpaid either in money or in power for their public services, beginning with the person invested with the royal authority and ending with the turnkey who extorts his last shilling from his starving prisoner; all members of the House of Lords who tremble lest the annihilation of their borough interest might not involve the risk of their hereditary legislative power and of those distinctions which considered in a pecuniary point of view are injurious to those beyond the pale of their caste in proportion as they are beneficial to those within; an immense majority of the assembly called the House of Commons, who would be reduced, if they desired to administer public business, to consult the interest of their electors and conform themselves. The functionaries who know that their claims to several millions yearly of the produce of the soil for the services of certain dogmas, which if necessary other men would enforce as effectually for as many thousands, would undergo a very severe examination [in the event of general Reform]. These persons propose to us the dilemma of submitting to a despotism which is notoriously gathering like an avalanche year by year, or taking the risk of something which it must be confessed bears the aspect of revolution. To this alternative we are reduced by the selfishness ...

[*The following passage is omitted in Mary Shelley's transcription:* It is of no avail that they call this selfishness principle or that they are self-deluded by the same sophism with which they would deceive others. To attach another name to the same idea to which those principles which demand the advantage of the greater number are admitted to appeal may puzzle the hearer but can in no manner change the import of it. But these, even should they be few would yet be few among the many.]

... of those who taunt us with it. And the history of the world teaches us not to hesitate an instant in the decision, if indeed the power of decision be not already past.

The establishment of King William III on the throne of England has already been referred to as a compromise between liberty and despotism. The Parliament of which that event was the act had ceased to be in an emphatic sense a representation of the people. The Long Parliament, questionless, was the organ of all classes of people in England since it effected the complete revolution in a tyranny consecrated by time. But since its meeting and since its dissolution a great change had taken place in England. Feudal manners and institutions having become obliterated, monopolies and patents having been abolished, property and personal liberty having been rendered secure, the nation advanced rapidly towards the acquirement of the elements of national prosperity. Population increased, a greater number of hands were employed in the labours of agriculture and commerce, towns arose where villages had been, and the proportion borne by those whose labour produces the materials of subsistence and enjoyment to those who claim for themselves a superfluity of these materials began to increase indefinitely. A fourth class therefore appeared in the nation, the unrepresented multitude. Nor was it so much that villages which sent no members to Parliament became great cities, and that towns which had been considerable enough to send members dwindled from local circumstances into villages. This cause no doubt contributed to the general effect of rendering the Commons House a less complete representation of the people. Yet had this been all, though it had ceased to be a legal and actual, it might still have been a virtual representation of the people. But the nation universally became multiplied into a denomination which had no constitutional presence in the state. This denomination had not existed before, or had existed only to a degree in which its interests were sensibly interwoven with that of those who enjoyed a constitutional presence. Thus, the proportion borne by the Englishmen who possessed [the] faculty of suffrage to those who were excluded from that faculty at the several periods of 1641 and 1688 had changed by the operation of these causes from 1 to 8 to 1 to 20. The rapid and effectual progress by which it changed from 1 to 20 to one to many hundreds in the interval between 1688 and 1819 is a process, to those familiar with history of the political economy of that period, which is rendered by these principles sufficiently intelligible. The number therefore of those who have influence on the government, even if numerically the same as at the former period, was relatively different. And a sufficiently just measure is afforded of the degree in which a country is enslaved or free by the consideration of the relative number of individuals who are admitted to the exercise of political rights. Meanwhile another cause was operating of a deeper and more extensive nature. The *class* who compose the Lords must, by the advantage of their situation as the great landed proprietors, possess a considerable influence over nomination to the Commons. This influence from an original imperfection in the equal distribution of suffrage was always enormous, but it is only since it has been combined with the cause before stated that it has appeared to be fraught with consequences incompatible with public liberty. In 1641 this influence was almost wholly [inoperative to] pervert the counsels of the nation from its own advantage. But at that epoch the enormous tyranny of the agents of the royal power weighed equally upon all denominations of men and united all counsels to extinguish it; add to which, the nation was as stated before in a very considerable degree fairly represented in Parliament. [The] common danger which was the bond of union between the aristocracy and the people having been destroyed, the former systematised their influence through the permanence of hereditary right, while the latter were losing power by the inflexibility of the institutions which forbade a just accommodation to their numerical increase.

After the operations of these causes had commenced, the accession of William III placed a seal upon forty years of Revolution.

The government of this country at the period of 1688 was regal, tempered by aristocracy, for what conditions of democracy attach to an assembly one portion of which [was] imperfectly nominated by less than a twentieth part of the people, and another perfectly nominated by the nobles? For the nobility, having by the assistance of the people imposed close limitations upon the royal power, finding that power to be its natural ally and the people (for the people from the increase of their numbers acquired greater and more important rights while the organ through which those rights might be asserted grew feebler in proportion to the increase of the cause of those rights and of their importance) its natural enemy, made the Crown the mask and pretence of their own authority. At this period began that despotism of the oligarchy of party, and under colour of administering the executive power lodged in the king, represented in truth the interests of the rich. When it is said by political reasoners, speaking of the interval between 1688 and the present time, that the royal power progressively increased, they use an expression which suggests a very imperfect and partial idea. The power which has increased is that entrusted with the administration of affairs, composed of men responsible to the aristocratic assemblies, or to the reigning party in those assemblies which represents those orders of the nation which are privileged, and will retain power as long as it pleases them and must be divested of power as soon as it ceases to please them. The power which has increased therefore is the [pow]er of the rich. The name and office of king is merely a mask of this power and is a kind of stalking-horse used to conceal these 'catchers of men,' while they lay their nets. Monarchy is only the string which ties the robber's bundle. Though less contumelious and abhorrent from the dignity of human nature than an absolute monarchy, an oligarchy of this nature exacts more of suffering from the people because it reigns both by opinion generated by imposture and the force which that opinion places within its grasp.

At the epoch adverted to, the device of public credit was first systematically applied as an instrument of government. It was employed at the accession of William III less as a resource for meeting the financial exigencies of the state than as a bond to connect those in the possession of property with those who had, by taking advantage of an accident of party, acceded to power. In the interval elapsed since that period it has accurately fulfilled the intention of its establishment and has continued to add strength to the government even until the present crisis. Now this advice is one of those execrable contrivances of misrule which overbalance the materials of common advantage produced by the progress of civilisation and increase the number of those who are idle in proportion to those who work, while it increases, through the factitious wants of those indolent, privileged persons, the quantity of work to be done. The rich, no longer being able to rule by force, have invented this scheme that they may rule by fraud.

The most despotic governments of antiquity were strangers to this invention, which is a compendious method of extorting from the people far more than praetorian guards and arbitrary tribunals and excise officers, created judges in the last resort, could ever wring. Neither the Persian monarchy nor the Roman Empire, where the will of one person was acknowledged as unappealable law, ever extorted a twentieth part the proportion now extorted from the property and labour of the inhabitants of Great Britain. The precious metals have been from the earliest records of civilisation employed as the signs of labour and the titles to an unequal distribution of its produce. The [government of] a country is necessarily entrusted with the affixing to certain portions of these metals a stamp by which to mark their genuineness; no other is considered as current coin, nor can be legal tender. The reason for this is that no alloyed coin should pass current and thereby depreciate the genuine and by augmenting the price of the articles which are the produce of labour, defraud the holders of that which is genuine of the advantages legally belonging to them. If the government itself abuses the trust reposed in it to debase the coin in order that it may derive advantage from the unlimited multiplication of the mark entitling the holder to command the labour and property of others, the gradations by which it sinks, as labour rises, to the level of their comparative values, produces public confusion and misery. The foreign exchange meanwhile instructs the government how temporary was its resource. This mode of making the distribution of the sign of labour a source of private aggrandisement at the expense of public confusion and loss was not wholly unknown to the nations of antiquity.

But the modern scheme of public credit is a far subtler and more complicated contrivance of misrule. All great transactions of personal property in England are managed by signs and that is by the authority of the possessor expressed upon paper, thus representing in a compendious form his right to so much gold, which represents his right to so much labour. A man may write on a piece of paper what he pleases; he may say he is worth a thousand when he is not worth a hundred pounds. If he can make others believe this, he has credit for the sum to which his name is attached. And so long as this credit lasts, he can enjoy all the advantages which would arise out of the actual possession of the sum he is believed to possess. He can lend two hundred to this man and three to that other, and his bills, among those who believe that he possesses this sum, pass like money. Of course in the same proportion as bills of this sort, beyond the actual goods or gold and silver possessed by the drawer, pass current, they defraud those who have gold and silver and goods of the advantages legally attached to the possession of them, and they defraud the labourer and artisan of the advantage attached to increasing the nominal price of labour, and such a participation in them as their industry *might* command, while they render wages fluctuating and add to the toil of the cultivator and manufacturer.

The existing government of England in substituting a currency of paper [for] one of gold has had no need to depreciate the currency by alloying the coin of the country; they have merely fabricated pieces of paper on which they promise to pay a certain sum. The holders of these papers came for payment in some representation of property universally exchangeable. They then declared that the persons who held the office for that payment could not be forced by

54   **SHELLEY**

law to pay. They declared subsequently that these pieces of paper were the legal coin of the country. Of this nature are all such transactions of companies and banks as consist in the circulation of promissory notes to a greater amount than the actual property possessed by those whose names they bear. They have the effect of augmenting the prices of provision and of benefiting at the expense of the community the speculators in this traffic. One of the vaunted effects of this system is to increase the national industry: that is, to increase the labours of the poor and those luxuries of the rich which they supply; to make a manufacturer work sixteen hours where he only worked eight; to turn children into lifeless and bloodless machines at an age when otherwise they would be at play before the cottage doors of their parents; to augment indefinitely the proportion of those who enjoy the profit of the labour of others as compared with those who exercise this labour ...

The consequences of this transaction have been the establishment of a new aristocracy, which has its basis in fraud as the old one has its basis in force. The hereditary landowners in England derived their title from royal grants—they are fiefs bestowed by conquerors, or church-lands, or they have been bought by bankers and merchants from those persons. Now bankers and merchants are persons whose ... Since usage has consecrated the distinction of the word aristocracy from its primitive meaning ... Let me be assumed to employ the word *aristocracy* in that ordinary sense which signifies that class of persons who possess a right to the produce of the labour of others, without dedicating to the common service any labour in return. This class of persons, whose existence is a prodigious anomaly in the social system, has ever constituted an inseparable portion of it, and there has never been an approach in practice towards any plan of political society modelled on equal justice, at least in the complicated mechanism of modern life. Mankind seem to acquiesce, as in a necessary condition of the imbecility of their own will and reason, in the existence of an aristocracy. With reference to this imbecility, it has doubtless been the instrument of great social advantage, although that advantage would have been greater which might have been produced according to the forms of a just distribution of the goods and evils of life. The object therefore of all enlightened legislation and administration is to enclose within the narrowest practicable limits this order of drones. The effect of the financial impostures of the modern rulers of England has been to increase the numbers of the drones. Instead of one aristocracy the condition [to] which, in the present state of human affairs, the friends of justice and liberty are willing to subscribe as to an inevitable evil, they have supplied us with two aristocracies: the one, consisting [of] great land proprietors and merchants who receive and interchange the produce of this country with the produce of other countries; in this, because all other great communities have as yet acquiesced in it, we acquiesce. Connected with the members of [it] is a certain generosity and refinement of manners and opinion which, although neither philosophy nor virtue has been that acknowledged substitute for them, which at least is a religion which makes respected those venerable names. The other is an aristocracy of attorneys and excisemen and directors and government pensioners, usurers, stock jobbers, country bankers, with their dependents and descendants. These are a set of pelting wretches in whose employment there is nothing to exercise, even to their distortion, the more majestic faculties of the soul. Though at the bottom it is all trick, there is something frank and magnificent in the chivalrous disdain of infamy connected with a gentleman. There is something to which—until you see through the base falsehood upon which all inequality is founded—it is difficult for the imagination to refuse its respect in the faithful and direct dealings of the substantial merchant. But in the habits and lives of this new aristocracy created out of an increase [in] the public calamities, and whose existence must be determined by their termination, there is nothing to qualify our disapprobation. They eat and drink and sleep and, in the intervals of those things performed with most ridiculous ceremony and accompaniments, they cringe and lie. They poison the literature of the age in which they live by requiring either the antitype of their own mediocrity in books, or such stupid and distorted and inharmonious idealisms as alone have the power to stir their torpid imaginations. Their hopes and fears are of the narrowest description. Their domestic affections are feeble, and they have no others. They think of any commerce with their species but as a means, never as an end, and as a means to the basest forms of personal advantage.

If this aristocracy had arisen from a false and depreciated currency to the exclusion of the other, its existence would have been a moral calamity and disgrace, but it would not have constituted an oppression. But the hereditary aristocracy who held the political administration of affairs took the measures which created this other for purposes peculiarly its own. Those measures were so contrived as in no manner to diminish the wealth and power of the contrivers. The lord does not spare himself one luxury, but the peasant and artisan are assured of many needful things. To support the system of social order according to its supposed unavoidable constitution, those from whose labour all those external accommodations which distinguish a civilised being from a savage arise, worked, before the institution of this double aristocracy, eight hours. And of these only the healthy were compelled to labour, the efforts of the old, the sick, and the immature being dispensed with, and they maintained by the labour of the sane, for such is the plain English of the poor-rates. That labour procured a competent share of the decencies of life, and society seemed to extend the benefits of its institution even to its most unvalued instruments. Although deprived of those resources of sentiment and knowledge which might have been their lot could the wisdom of the institutions of social forms have established a system of strict justice, yet they earned by their labour a competency in those external materials of life which, and not the loss of moral and intellectual excellence, is supposed to be the legitimate object of the desires and murmurs of the poor. Since the institution of this double aristocracy, however, they have often worked not ten but twenty hours a day. Not that all the poor have rigidly worked twenty hours, but that the worth of the labour of twenty hours now, in food and clothing, is equivalent to the worth of ten hours then. And because twenty hours' labour cannot, from the nature of the human frame, be exacted from those who before performed ten, the aged and the sickly are compelled either to work or starve. Children who were exempted from labour are put in requisition, and the vigorous promise of the coming generation blighted by premature exertion. For fourteen hours' labour which they do perform, they receive—no matter in what nominal amount—the price of seven. They eat less bread, wear worse clothes, are more ignorant, immoral, miserable, and desperate. This, then, is the condition of the lowest and the largest class from whose labour the whole materials of life are wrought, of which the others are only the receivers or the consumers. They are more superstitious, for misery on earth begets a diseased expectation and panic-stricken faith in miseries beyond the grave. 'God,' they argue, 'rules this world as well as that; and assuredly since his nature is immutable, and his powerful will unchangeable, he rules them by the same laws.' The gleams of hope which speak of Paradise seem like the flames in Milton's hell only to make darkness visible, and all things take [their] colour from what surrounds them. They become revengeful . . .

But the condition of all classes of society, excepting those within the privileged pale, is singularly unprosperous, and even they experience the reaction of their own short-sighted tyranny in all those sufferings and deprivations which are not of a distinctly physical nature, in the loss of dignity, simplicity, and energy, and in the possession of all those qualities which distinguish a slave-driver from a proprietor. Right government being an institution for the purpose of securing such a moderate degree of happiness to men as has been experimentally practicable, the sure character of misgovernment is misery, and first discontent and, if that be despised, then insurrection, as the legitimate expression of that misery. The public ought to demand happiness; the labouring classes, when they cannot get food for their labour, are impelled to take it by force. Laws and assemblies and courts of justice and delegated powers placed in balance or in opposition are the means and the form, but public happiness is the substance and the end of political institution. Whenever this is attained in a nation, not from external force but from the internal arrangement and divisions of the common burthens of defence and maintenance, then there is oppression. And then arises an alternative between reform and the institution of a military despotism, or a revolution in which these two parties, one starving after ill-digested systems of democracy, and the other clinging to the outworn abuses of power, leave the few who aspire to more than the former and who would overthrow the latter at whatever expense to wait until that modified advantage which results from this conflict produces a small portion of that social improvement which, with the temperance and the toleration which both regard as a crime, might have resulted from the occasion which they let pass in a far more signal manner.

The propositions which are the consequences or the corollaries to which the preceding reasoning seems to have conducted us are:

That the majority [of] the people of England are destitute and miserable, ill-clothed, ill-fed, ill-educated.

That they know this, and that they are impatient to procure a reform of the cause of their abject and wretched state.

That the cause of this peculiar misery is the unequal distribution which, under the form of the national debt, has been surreptitiously made of the products of their labour and the products of the labour of their ancestors; for all property is the produce of labour.

That the cause of that cause is a defect in the government.

That if they knew nothing of their condition, but believed that all they endured and all [they] were deprived of arose from the unavoidable condition of human life, this belief being an error, and [one] the endurance of [which] enforces an injustice, every enlightened and honourable person, whatever may be the imagined interest of his peculiar class, ought to excite them to the discovery of the true state of the case and to the temperate but irresistible vindication of their rights.

It is better that they should be instructed in the whole truth, that they should see the clear grounds of their rights, the objects to which they ought to tend; and be impressed with the first persuasion that patience and reason and endurance, and a calm yet invisible progress ...

A reform in England is most just and necessary. What ought to be that reform?

A writer of the present day [Thomas Malthus] (a priest of course, for his doctrines are those of a eunuch and of a tyrant) has stated that the evils of the poor arise from an excess of population, and that after they have been stript naked by the tax-gatherer and reduced to bread and tea and fourteen hours of hard labour by their masters, and after the frost has bitten their defenceless limbs, and the cramp has wrung like a disease within their bones, and hunger—and the suppressed revenge of hunger—has stamped the ferocity of want like the mark of Cain upon their countenance, that the last tie by which Nature holds them to benignant earth whose plenty is garnered up in the strongholds of their tyrants, is to be divided; that the single alleviation of their sufferings and their scorns, the one thing which made it impossible to degrade them below the beasts, which amid all their crimes and miseries yet separated a cynical and unmanly contamination, an anti-social cruelty, from all soothing, elevating, and harmonious gentleness of the sexual intercourse and the humanising charities of domestic life which are its appendages—that this is to be obliterated. They are required to abstain from marrying under penalty of starvation. And it is threatened to deprive them of that property which is as strictly their birthright as a gentleman's land is his birthright, without giving them any compensation but the insulting advice to conquer, with minds undisciplined in the habits of higher gratification, a propensity which persons of the most consummate wisdom have been unable to resist, and which it is difficult to admire a person for having resisted. The doctrine of this writer is that the principle of population when under no dominion of moral restraint [is] outstripping the sustenance produced by the labour of man, and that not in proportion to the number of inhabitants, but operating equally in a thinly peopled community as in one where the population is enormous, being not a prevention but a check. So far a man might have been conducted by a train of reasoning which, though it may be shown to be defective, would argue in the reasoner no selfish and slavish feelings. But he has the hardened insolence to propose as a remedy that the poor should be compelled (for what except compulsion is a threat of the confiscation of those funds which by the institutions of their country had been set apart for their sustenance in sickness or destitution?) to abstain from sexual intercourse, while the rich are to be permitted to add as many mouths to consume the products of the labour of the poor as they please. The rights of all men are intrinsically and originally equal and they forgo the assertion of all of them only that they may the more securely enjoy a portion. If any new disadvantages are found to attach to the condition of social existence, those disadvantages ought not to be borne exclusively by one class of men, nor especially by that class whose ignorance leads them to exaggerate the advantages of sensual enjoyment, whose callous habits render domestic endearments more important to dispose them to resist the suggestions to violence and cruelty by which their situation ever exposes them to be tempted, and all whose other enjoyments are limited and few, while their sufferings are various and many. In this sense I cannot imagine how the advocates of equality would so readily have conceded that the unlimited operation of the principle of population affects the truth of these theories. On the contrary, the more heavy and certain are the evils of life, the more injustice is there in casting the burden of them exclusively on one order in the community. They seem to have conceded it merely because their opponents have insolently assumed it. Surely it is enough that the rich should possess to the exclusion of the poor all other luxuries and comforts, and wisdom, and refinement, the least envied but the most deserving of envy among all their privileges.

What is the reform that we desire? Before we aspire after theoretical perfection in the amelioration of our political state, it is necessary that we possess those advantages which we have been cheated of and to which the experience of modern times has proved that nations even under the present [conditions] are susceptible:

first, we would regain these; second, we would establish some form of government which might secure us against such a series of events as have conducted us to a persuasion that the forms according to which it is now administered are inadequate to that purpose.

We would abolish the national debt.

We would disband the standing army.

We would, with every possible regard to the existing interests of the holders, abolish sinecures.

We would, with every possible regard to the existing interests of the holders, abolish tithes, and make all religions, all forms of opinion respecting the origin and government of the universe, equal in the eye of the law.

We would make justice cheap, certain, and speedy, and extend the institution of juries to every possible occasion of jurisprudence.

The national debt was chiefly contracted in two libertine wars, undertaken by the privileged classes of the country—the first, for the ineffectual purpose of tyrannising over one portion of their subjects; the second, in order to extinguish the resolute spirit of obtaining their rights, in another. The labour which this money represents, and that which is represented by the money wrung, for purposes of the same detestable character, out of the people since the commencement of the American war would, if properly employed, have covered our land with monuments of architecture exceeding the sumptuousness and the beauty of Egypt and Athens; it might have made every peasant's cottage, surrounded with its garden, a little paradise of comfort, with every convenience desirable in civilised life; neat tables and chairs, and good beds, and a nice collection of useful books; and our ships manned by sailors well-paid and well-clothed might have kept watch round this glorious island against the less enlightened nations which assuredly would have envied, until they could have imitated, its prosperity. But the labour which is expressed by these sums has been diverted from these purposes of human happiness to the promotion of slavery, or the attempt at dominion, and a great portion of the sum in question is debt and must be paid. Is it to remain unpaid forever, an eternal rent-charge upon the sacred soil from which the inhabitants of these islands draw their subsistence? This were to pronounce the perpetual institution of two orders of aristocracy, and men are in a temper to endure one with some reluctance. Is it to be paid now? If so what are the funds, or when and how is it to be paid? The fact is that the national debt is a debt not contracted by the whole nation towards a portion of it, but a debt contracted by the whole mass of the privileged classes towards one particular portion of those classes. If the principal were paid, the whole property of those who possess property must be valued and the public creditor, whose property would have been included in this estimate, satisfied out of the proceeds. It has been said that all the land in the nation is mortgaged for the amount of the national debt. This is a partial statement; not only all the land in the nation but all the property of whatever denomination, all the houses and the furniture and the goods and every article of merchandise, and the property which is represented by the very money lent by the fund-holder, who is bound to pay a certain portion as debtor while he is to receive another certain portion as creditor. The property of the rich is mortgaged: to use the language of the law, let the mortgagee foreclose.

If the principal of this debt were paid, after such reductions had been made so as to make an equal value, taking corn for the standard, be given as was received, it would be the rich who alone could, as justly they ought to pay it. It would be a mere transfer among persons of property. Such a gentleman must lose a third of his estate, such a citizen a fourth of his money in the funds; the persons who borrowed would have paid, and the juggling and complicated system of paper finance be suddenly at an end. As it is, the interest is chiefly paid by those who had no hand in the borrowing and who are sufferers in other respects from the consequences of those transactions in which the money was spent.

The payment of the principal of what is called the national debt, which it is pretended is so difficult a problem, is only difficult to those who do not see who is the creditor and who the debtor, and who the wretched sufferers from whom they both wring taxes which under the form of interest is given by the former [latter] and accepted by the latter [former]. It is from the labour of those who have no property that all the persons who possess property think to extort the perpetual interest of a debt, the whole of them to the part, which the latter [former] know they could not persuade the former [latter] to pay, but by conspiring with them in an imposture which makes the third class pay what the first [second] neither received by their sanction nor spent for their benefit, and what the second [first] never lent to them. They would both shift to the labour of the present and of all succeeding generations the payment of the interest of their own debt, from themselves and their posterity, because the payment of the principal would be no more than a compromise and transfer of property between each other by which the nation would be spared forty-four millions a year, which now is paid to maintain in luxury and indolence the public debtors and to protect them from the demand of their creditors upon them, who, being part of the same body and owing as debtors while they possess a claim as creditors, agree to abstain from demanding the principal which they must all unite to pay, for the sake of receiving an enormous interest which is principally wrung out of those who had no concern whatever in the transaction. One of the first acts of a reformed government would undoubtedly be an effectual scheme for compelling these to compromise their debt between themselves.

When I speak of persons of property I mean not every man who possesses any right of property; I mean the rich. Every man whose scope in society has a plebeian and intelligible utility, whose personal exertions are more valuable to him than his capital; every tradesman who is not a monopolist, all surgeons and physicians and those mechanics and editors and literary men and artists, and farmers, all those persons whose profits spring from honourably and honestly exerting their own skill or wisdom or strength in greater abundance than from the employment of money to take advantage of the necessity of the starvation of their fellow citizens for their profit, or those who pay, as well as those more obviously understood by the labouring classes, the interest of the national debt. It is the interest of all these persons as well as that of the poor to insist upon the payment of the principal.

For this purpose the form ought to be as simple and succinct as possible. The operations deciding who was to pay, at what time, and how much, and to whom are divested of financial chicanery, problems readily to be determined. The common tribunals may possess a legal jurisdiction to award the proportion due upon the several claim of each.

There are two descriptions of property which, without entering into the subtleties of a more refined moral theory as applicable to the existing forms of society, are entitled to two very different measures of forbearance and regard. And this forbearance and regard have by political institutions usually been accorded in an inverse reason from what is just and natural. Labour, industry, economy, skill, genius, or any similar powers honourably and innocently exerted are the foundations of one description of property, and all true political institutions ought to defend every man in the exercise of his discretion with respect to property so acquired. Of this kind is the principal part of the property enjoyed by those who are but one degree removed from the class which subsists by daily labour. Yet there are instances of persons in this class who have procured their property by fraudulent and violent means, as there are instances in the other of persons who have acquired their property by innocent or honourable exertion. All political science abounds with limitations and exceptions. Property thus acquired men leave to their children. Absolute right becomes weakened by descent, first because it is only to avoid the greater evil of arbitrarily interfering with the discretion of any man in matters of property that the great evil of acknowledging any person to have an exclusive right to property who has not created it by his skill or labour is admitted, and secondly because the mode of its having been originally acquired is forgotten, and it is confounded with the property acquired in a very different manner; and the principle upon which all property justly rests, after the great principle of the general advantage, becomes thus disregarded and misunderstood. Yet the privilege of disposing of property by will is one necessarily connected with the existing forms of domestic life, and exerted merely by those who have acquired property by industry or who have preserved it by economy, would never produce any great and invidious inequality of fortune. A thousand accidents would perpetually tend to level the accidental elevation, and the signs of property would perpetually recur to those whose deserving skill might attract or whose labour might create it.

But there is another species of property which has its foundation in usurpation, or imposture, or violence, without which, by the nature of things, immense possessions of gold or land could never have been accumulated. Of this nature is the principal part of the property enjoyed by the aristocracy and by the great fund-holders, the great majority of whose ancestors never either deserved it by their skill and talents or acquired and created it by their personal labour. It could not be that they deserved it, for if the honourable exertion of the most glorious imperial faculties of our nature had been the criterion of the possession of property, the posterity of Shakespeare, of Milton, of Hampden, of Lor[d Bacon] would be the wealthiest proprietors in England. It could not be that they acquired it by legitimate industry, for, besides that the real mode of acquisition is matter of history, no honourable profession or honest trade, nor the hereditary exercise of it, ever in such numerous instances accumulated masses of property so vast as those enjoyed by the ruling orders in England. They were either grants from the feudal sovereigns whose right to what they granted was founded upon conquest or oppression, both a denial of all right; or they were the lands of the ancient Catholic clergy which, according to the most acknowledged principles of public justice, reverted to the nation at their suppression, or they were the products of patents and monopolies, an exercise of sovereignty most pernicious that direct violence to the interests of a commercial nation; or in later times such property has been accumulated by dishonourable cunning and the taking advantage of a fictitious paper currency to obtain an unfair power over labour and the fruits of labour.

Property thus accumulated being transmitted from father to son acquires, as property of the more legitimate kind loses, force and sanction, but in a more limited manner. For not only on an examination and recurrence to first principles is it seen to have been founded on a violation of all that to which the latter owes its sacredness, but it is felt in its existence and perpetuation as a public burthen, and known as a rallying point to the ministers of tyranny, having the property of a snowball, gathering as it rolls, and rolling until it bursts. [It] is astonishing that political theorists have not branded [it] as the most pernicious and odious. [Yet] there are three sets of people, one who can place a thing to another in an intelligible light, another who can understand it when so communicated, and a third who can neither discover [n]or understand it.

Labour and skill and the immediate wages of labour and skill is a property of the most sacred and indisputable right and the foundation of all other property. And the right of a man [to] property in the exertion of his own bodily and mental faculties, or to the produce and free reward from and for that exertion is the most [inalienable of rights]. If, however, he takes by violence or appropriates to himself through fraudulent cunning, or receives from another property so acquired, his claim to that property is of a far inferior force. We may acquiesce, if we evidently perceive an overbalance of public advantage in submission under this claim; but if any public emergency should arise, at which it might be necessary as at present by a tax on capital to satisfy the claims of a part of the nation by a contribution from such national resources as may with the least injustice be appropriated to that purpose, assuredly it would not be on labour and skill, the foundation of all property, nor on the profits and savings of labour and skill, which are property itself, but on such possession which can only be called property in a modified sense, as have from their magnitude and their nature an evident origin in violence or imposture.

The national debt, as has been stated, is a debt contracted by the whole of a particular class in the nation towards a portion of that class. It is sufficiently clear that this debt was not contracted for the purpose of the public advantage. Besides there was no authority in the nation competent to a measure of this nature. The usual vindication of national debts is that, [since] they are contracted in an overwhelming measure for the purpose of defence against a common danger, for the vindication of the rights and liberties of posterity, it is just that posterity should bear the burthen of payment. This reasoning is most fallacious. The history of nations presents us with a succession of extraordinary emergencies, and through their present imperfect organisation their existence is perpetually threatened by new and unexpected combinations and developments of foreign or internal force. Imagine a situation of equal emergency to occur to England as that which the ruling party assume to have occurred as their excuse for burthening the nation with the perpetual payment of £45,000,000 annually. Suppose France, Russia, and America were to enter into a league against England, the first to revenge [avenge] its injuries, the second to satisfy its ambition, the third to soothe its jealousy. Could the nation bear £90,000,000 of yearly interest? Must there be twice as many luxurious and idle persons? Must the labourer receive for twenty-eight hours' work what he now receives for fourteen, as he now receives for fourteen what he once received for seven? But this argument . . .

What is meant by a reform of Parliament? If England were a republic governed by one assembly; if there were no chamber of hereditary aristocracy which is at once an actual and a virtual representation of all who claim through rank or wealth superiority over their countrymen; if there were no king who is as the rallying point of those whose tendency is at once to [gather] and to confer that power which is consolidated at the expense of the nation, then

. . .

The advocates of universal suffrage have reasoned correctly that no individual who is governed can be denied a direct share in the government of his country without supreme justice. If we pursue the train of reasonings which have conducted to this conclusion, we discover that systems of social order still more incompatible than universal suffrage with any reasonable hope of instant accomplishment appear to be that which should result from a just combination of the elements of social life. I do not understand why those reasoners who propose at any price an immediate appeal to universal suffrage, because it is that which it is injustice to withhold, do not insist on the same ground on the immediate abolition, for instance, of monarchy and aristocracy, and the levelling of inordinate wealth, and an agrarian distribution, including the parks and chases of the rich, of the uncultivated districts of the country. No doubt the institution of universal suffrage would by necessary consequence *immediately* tend to the *temporary* abolition of these forms; because it is impossible that the people, having attained power, should fail to see what the demagogues now conceal from them the legitimate consequence of the doctrines through which they had attained it. A republic, however just in its principle and glorious in its object, would through violence and sudden change which must attend it incur a great risk of being as rapid in its decline as in its growth. It is better that they should be instructed in the whole truth; that they should see the clear grounds of their rights, the objects to which they ought to tend; and be impressed with the just persuasion that patience and reason and endurance [are the means of] a calm yet irresistible progress. A civil war, which might be engendered by the passions attending on this mode of reform, would confirm in the mass of the nation those military habits which have been already introduced by our tyrants and with which liberty is incompatible. From the moment that a man is a soldier, he becomes a slave. He is taught obedience; his will is no longer, which is the most sacred prerogative of man, guided by his own judgement. He is taught to despise human life and human suffering; this is the universal distinction of slaves. He is more degraded than a murderer; he is like the bloody knife which has stabbed and feels not; a murderer we may abhor and despise, a soldier is by profession beyond abhorrence and below contempt.

Chapter 3

PROBABLE MEANS

That Commons should reform itself, uninfluenced by any fear that the people would, on their refusal, assume to itself that office, seems a contradiction. What need of reform if it expresses the will and watches over the interests of the public? And if, as is sufficiently evident, it despises that will and neglects that interest, what motives would incite it to institute a reform which the aspect of the times renders indeed sufficiently perilous, but without which there will speedily be no longer anything in England to distinguish it from the basest and most abject community of slaves that ever existed.

The great principle of reform consists in every individual of mature age and perfect understanding giving his consent to the institution and the continued existence of the social system which is instituted for his advantage and for the advantage of others in his situation. As in a great nation this is practically impossible, masses of individuals consent to qualify other individuals, whom they delegate to superintend their concerns. These delegates have constitutional authority to exercise the functions of sovereignty;

they unite in the highest degree the legislative and executive functions. A government that is founded on any other basis is a government of fraud or force and ought on the first convenient occasion to be overthrown. The broad principle of political reform is the natural equality of men, not with relation to their property but to their rights. That equality in possessions which Jesus Christ so passionately taught is a moral rather than political truth and is such as social institutions cannot without mischief inflexibly secure. Morals and politics can only be considered as portions of the same science, with relation to a system of such absolute perfection as Christ and Plato and Rousseau and other reasoners have asserted, and as Godwin has, with irresistible eloquence, systematised and developed. Equality in possessions must be the last result of the utmost refinements of civilisation; it is one of the conditions of that system of society towards which with whatever hope of ultimate success, it is our duty to tend. We may and ought to advert to it as to the elementary principle, as to the goal, unattainable perhaps by us, but which, as it were, we revive in our posterity to pursue. We derive tranquillity and courage and grandeur of soul from contemplating an object which is, because we will it, and may be because we hope and desire it, and must be if succeeding generations of the enlightened sincerely and earnestly seek it. We should with sincere and patient as ...

But our present business is with the difficult and unbending realities of actual life, and when we have drawn inspiration from the great object of our hopes it becomes us with patience and resolution to apply ourselves to accommodating our theories to immediate practice.

That representative assembly called the House of Commons ought questionless to be *immediately* nominated by the great mass of the people. The aristocracy and those who unite in their own persons the vast privileges conferred by the possession of inordinate wealth are sufficiently represented by the House of Peers and by the King. Those theorists who admire and would put into action the mechanism of what is called the British Constitution would acquiesce in this view of the question. For if the House of Peers be a permanent representative of the privileged classes, if the regal power be no more than another form and a form still more jealously to be regarded, of the same representation, while the House of Commons be not chosen by the mass of the population, what becomes of that democratic element, upon the presence of which it has been supposed that the waning superiority of England over the surrounding nations has depended?

Any sudden attempt at universal suffrage would produce an immature attempt at a republic. It [is better] that [an] object so inexpressibly great and sacred should never have been attempted than that it should be attempted and fail. It is no prejudice to the ultimate establishment of the boldest political innovations that we temporise so as, when they shall be accomplished, they may be rendered permanent.

Considering the population of Great Britain and Ireland as twenty millions and the representative assembly as five hundred, each member ought to be the expression of the will of 40,000 persons; of these two-thirds would [consist of] women and children and persons under age; the actual number of voters therefore for each member would be 13,333. The whole extent of the empire might be divided into five hundred electoral departments or parishes, and the inhabitants assemble on a certain day to exercise their rights of suffrage.

Mr Bentham and other writers have urged the admission of females to the right of suffrage; this attempt seems somewhat immature. Should my opinion be the result of despondency, the writer of these pages would be the last to withhold his vote from any system which might tend to an equal and full development of the capacities of all living beings.

The system of voting by ballot which some reasoners have recommended is attended with obvious inconveniences. [It withdraws the elector from the regard of his country, and] his neighbours, and permits him to conceal the motives of his vote, which, if concealed, cannot but be dishonourable; when, if he had known that he had to render a public account of his conduct, he would never have permitted them to guide him. There is in this system of voting by ballot and of electing a member of the *Representative Assembly* as a churchwarden is elected something too mechanical. The elector and the elected ought to meet one another face to face and interchange the meanings of actual presence and share some common impulses and, in a degree, understand each other. There ought to be the common sympathy of the excitements of a popular assembly among the electors themselves. The imagination would thus be strongly excited, and a mass of generous and enlarged and popular sentiments be awakened, which would give the vitality of . . .

That republican boldness of censuring and judging one another, which has indeed [been] exerted in England under the title of 'public opinion,' though perverted from its true uses into an instrument of prejudice and calumny, would then be applied to its genuine purposes. Year by year the people would become more susceptible of assuming forms of government more simple and beneficial.

It is in this publicity of the exercise of sovereignty that the difference between the republics of Greece and the monarchies of Asia consisted. The actions of the times . . .

If the existing government shall compel the nation to take the task of reform into its own hands, one of the most obvious consequences of such a circumstance would be the abolition of monarchy and aristocracy. Why, it will then be argued, if the subsisting condition of social forms is to be thrown into confusion, should these things be endured? Then why do we now endure them? Is it because we think that an hereditary King is cheaper and wiser than an elected President, or a House of Lords and a Bench of Bishops are institutions modelled by the wisdom of the most refined and civilised periods, beyond which the wit of mortal man can furnish nothing more perfect? In case the subsisting government should compel the people to revolt to establish a representative assembly in defiance of them and to assume in that assembly an attitude of resistance and defence, this question would probably be answered in a very summary manner. No friend of mankind and of his country can desire that such a crisis should suddenly arrive; but still less, once having arrived, can he hesitate under what banner to array his person and his power. At the peace, the people would have been contented with strict economy and severe retrenchment, and some direct and intelligible plan for producing that equilibrium between the capitalists and the landholders which is delusively styled the payment of the national debt; had this system been adopted, they probably would have refrained from exacting Parliamentary reform, the only secure guarantee that it would have been pursued. Two years ago it might still have been possible to have commenced a system of gradual reform. The people were then insulted, tempted, and betrayed, and *the petitions of a million* of men rejected with disdain. Now they are more miserable, more hopeless, more impatient of their misery. Above all, they have become more universally aware of the true sources of their misery. It is possible that the period of conciliation is past, and that after having played with the confidence and cheated the expectations of the people, their passions will be too little under discipline to allow them to wait the slow, gradual, and certain operation of such a reform as we can imagine the constituted authorities to concede.

Upon the issue of this question depends the species of reform which a philosophical mind should regard with approbation. If reform shall be begun by the existing government, let us be contented with a limited *beginning*, with any whatsoever opening; let the rotten boroughs be disfranchised and their rights transferred to the unrepresented cities and districts of the nation; it is no matter how slow, gradual, and cautious be the change; we shall demand more and more with firmness and moderation, never anticipating, but never deferring the moment of successful opposition, so that the people may become habituated [to] exercising the functions of sovereignty, in proportion as they acquire the possession of it. If reform could begin from within the Houses of Parliament, as constituted at present, it appears to me that what is called moderate reform, that is a suffrage whose qualification should be the possession of a certain small property, and triennial parliaments, would be principles—a system in which, for the sake of obtaining without bloodshed or confusion ulterior improvements of a more important character, all reformers ought to acquiesce. Not that such are first principles, or that they would produce a system of perfect social institutions or one approaching to [such]. But nothing is more idle than to reject a limited benefit because we cannot without great sacrifices obtain an unlimited one. We might thus reject a representative republic, if it were obtainable, on the plea that the imagination of man can conceive of something more absolutely perfect. Towards whatsoever we regard as perfect, undoubtedly it is no less our duty than it is our nature to press forward; this is the generous enthusiasm which accomplishes not indeed the consummation after which it aspires, but one which approaches it in a degree far nearer than if the whole powers had not been developed by a delusion. It is in politics rather than in religion that faith is meritorious.

If the Houses of Parliament obstinately and perpetually refuse to concede any reform to the people, my vote is for universal suffrage and equal representation. My vote is—but, it is asked, how shall this be accomplished, in defiance of and in opposition to the constituted authorities of the nation, they who possess whether with or without its consent the command of a standing army and of a legion of spies and police officers and hold all the strings of that complicated mechanism with which the hopes and fears of men are moved like puppets? They would disperse any assembly really chosen by the people; they would shoot and hew down any multitude without regard to sex or age as the Jews did the Canaanites, which might be collected in its defence; they would calumniate, imprison, starve, ruin, and expatriate every person who wrote or acted, or thought, or might be suspected to think against them; misery and extermination would fill the country from one end to another ...

This question I would answer by another.

Will you endure to pay the half of your earnings to maintain in luxury and idleness the confederation of your tyrants as the reward of a successful conspiracy to defraud and oppress you? Will you make your tame cowardice and the branding record of it the everlasting inheritance of your posterity? Not only this: will you render by your torpid endurance this condition of things as permanent as the system of castes in India by which the same horrible injustice is perpetrated under another form?

Assuredly no Englishmen by whom these propositions are understood will answer in the affirmative; and the opposite side of the alternative remains.

When the majority in any nation arrive at a conviction that it is their duty and their interest to divest the minority of a power employed to their disadvantage, and the minority are sufficiently mistaken as to believe that their superiority is tenable, a struggle must ensue.

If the majority are enlightened, united, impelled by a uniform enthusiasm and animated by a distinct and powerful apprehension of their object—and full confidence in their undoubted power—the struggle is merely nominal. The minority perceive the approaches of the development of an irresistible force. By the influence of the public opinion of their weakness on those political forms of which no government but an absolute despotism is devoid. They divest themselves of their usurped distinctions; the public tranquillity is not disturbed by the revolution.

But these conditions may only be imperfectly fulfilled by the state of a people grossly oppressed and impotent to cast off the load. Their enthusiasm may have been subdued by the killing weight of toil and suffering; they may be panic-stricken and disunited by their oppressors and the demagogues, the influence of fraud may have been sufficient to weaken the union of classes which compose them by suggesting jealousies, and the position of the conspirators, although it is to be forced by repeated assaults, may be tenable until the siege can be vigorously urged. The true patriot will endeavour to enlighten and to unite the nation and animate it with enthusiasm and confidence. For this purpose he will be indefatigable in promulgating political truth. He will endeavour to rally round one standard the divided friends of liberty and make them forget the subordinate objects with regard to which they differ by appealing to that respecting which they are all agreed. He will promote such open confederations among men of principle and spirit as may tend to make their intentions and their efforts converge to a common centre. He will discourage all secret associations which have a tendency, by making national will develop itself in a partial and premature manner, to cause tumult and confusion. He will urge the necessity of exciting the people frequently to exercise their right of assembling in such limited numbers as that all present may be actual parties to the proceedings of the day. Lastly, if circumstances had collected a more considerable number as at Manchester on the memorable 16th of August [1819], if the tyrants command their troops to fire upon them or cut them down unless they disperse, he will exhort them peaceably to risk the danger, and to expect without resistance the onset of the cavalry, and wait with folded arms the event of the fire of the artillery and receive with unshrinking bosoms the bayonets of the charging battalions. Men are every day persuaded to incur greater perils for a less manifest advantage. And this, not because active resistance is not justifiable when all other means shall have failed, but because in this instance temperance and courage would produce greater advantages than the most decisive victory. In the first place the soldiers are men and Englishmen, and it is not to be believed that they would massacre an unresisting multitude of their countrymen drawn up in unarmed array before them and bearing in their looks the calm, deliberate resolution to perish rather than abandon the assertion of their rights. In the confusion of flight the ideas of the soldier become confused and he massacres those who fly from him by the instinct of his trade. In the struggle of conflict and resistance he is irritated by a sense of his own danger; he is flattered by an apprehension of his magnanimity in incurring it; he considers the blood of his countrymen at once the price of his valour, the pledge of his security. He applauds himself by reflecting that these base and dishonourable motives will gain him credit among his comrades and his officers, who are animated by the same as if they were something the same. But if he should observe neither resistance nor flight he would be reduced to impotence and indecision. Thus far, his ideas were governed by the same law as those of a dog who chases a flock of sheep to the corner of the field and keeps aloof when they make the firm parade of resistance. But the soldier is a man and an Englishman. This unexpected reception would probably throw him back upon a recollection of the true nature of the measures of which he was made an instrument, and the enemy might be converted into the ally.

The patriot will be foremost to publish the boldest truths in the most fearless manner, yet without the slightest tincture of personal malignity. He would encourage all others to the same efforts and assist them to the utmost of his power with the resources both of his intellect and fortune. He would call upon them to despise imprisonment and persecution and lose no opportunity of bringing public opinion and the power of the tyrants into circumstances of perpetual contest and opposition.

All might, however, be ineffectual to produce so uniform an impulse of the national will as to preclude a further struggle. The strongest argument, perhaps, for the necessity of reform is the inoperative and unconscious abjectness to which the purposes of a considerable mass of the people are reduced. They neither know nor care. They are sinking into a resemblance with the Hindoos and the Chinese, who were once men as they are. Unless the cause which renders them passive subjects instead of active citizens be removed, they will sink with accelerated gradations into that barbaric and unnatural civilisation which destroys all the differences among men. It is in vain to exhort us to wait until all men shall desire freedom whose real interest will consist in its establishment. It is in vain to hope to enlighten them while their tyrants employ the utmost artifices of all their complicated engine to perpetuate the infection of every species of fanaticism and error from generation to generation. The advocates of reform ought indeed to leave no effort unexerted, and they ought to be indefatigable in exciting all men to examine.

But if they wait until those neutral politicians, a class whose opinions represent the actions of this class, are persuaded that so soon [as] effectual reform is necessary, the occasion will have passed or will never arrive, and the people will have exhausted their strength in ineffectual expectation and will have sunk into incurable supineness. It was principally the [effect of] a similar quietism that the populous and extensive nations of Asia have fallen into their existing decrepitude; and that anarchy, insecurity, ignorance, and barbarism, the symptoms of the confirmed disease of monarchy, have reduced nations of the most delicate physical and intellectual organisation and under the most fortunate climates of the globe to a blank in the history of man. The manufacturers to a man are persuaded of the necessity of reform; an immense majority of the inhabitants of London ...

The reasoners who incline to the opinion that it is not sufficient that the innovators should produce a majority in the nation, but that we ought to expect such an unanimity as would preclude anything amounting to a serious dispute, are prompted to this view of the question by the dread of anarchy and massacre. Infinite and inestimable calamities belong to oppression, but the most fatal of them all is that mine of unexploded mischief which it has practised beneath the foundations of society, and with which, 'pernicious to one touch' it threatens to involve the ruin of the entire building together with its own. But delay merely renders these mischiefs more tremendous, not the less inevitable. For the utmost may now be the crisis of the social disease [which] is rendered thus periodical, chronic, and incurable.

The savage brutality of the populace is proportioned to the arbitrary character of their government, and tumults and insurrections soon, as in Constantinople, become consistent with the permanence of the causing evil, of which they might have been the critical determination.

The public opinion in England ought first to [be] excited to action, and the durability of those forms within which the oppressors intrench themselves brought perpetually to the test of its operation. No law or institution can last if this opinion be distinctly pronounced against it. For this purpose government ought to be defied, in cases of questionable result, to prosecute for political libel. All questions relating to the jurisdiction of magistrates and courts of law respecting which any doubt could be raised ought to be agitated with indefatigable pertinacity. Some two or three of the popular leaders have shown the best spirit in this respect; they only want system and co-operation. The tax-gatherer ought to be compelled in every practicable instance to distrain while the right to impose taxes, as was the case in the beginning of the resistance to tyranny of Charles I, is formally contested by an overwhelming multitude of defendants before the courts of common law. Confound the subtlety of lawyers with the subtlety of the law. All of the nation would thus be excited to develop itself and to declare whether it acquiesced in the existing forms of government. The manner in which all questions of this nature might be decided would develop the occasions and afford a prognostic as to the success of more decisive measures. Simultaneously with this active and vigilant system of opposition means ought to be taken of solemnly conveying the sense of large bodies and various denominations of the people in a manner the most explicit to the existing depositories of power. Petitions, couched in the actual language of the petitioners, and emanating from distinct assemblies ought to load the tables of the House of Commons. The poets, philosophers, and artists ought to remonstrate, and the memorials entitled their petitions might show the diversity [of] convictions they entertain of the inevitable connection between national prosperity and freedom, and the cultivation of the imagination and the cultivation of scientific truth, and the profound development of moral and metaphysical enquiry. Suppose these memorials to be severally written by Godwin, Hazlitt, Bentham, and Hunt, they would be worthy of the age and of the cause; these, radiant and irresistible like the meridian sun, would strike all but the eagles who dared to gaze upon its beams, with blindness and confusion. These appeals of solemn and emphatic argument from those who have already a predestined existence among posterity would appal the enemies of mankind by their echoes from every corner of the world in which the majestic literature of England is cultivated; it would be like a voice from beyond the dead of those who will live in the memories of men, when they must be forgotten; it would be Eternity warning Time.

Let us hope that at this stage of the progress of reform, the oppressors would feel their impotence and reluctantly and imperfectly concede some limited portion of the rights of the people and disgorge some morsels of their undigested prey. In this case the people ought to be exhorted by everything ultimately dear to them to pause until by the exercise of those rights which they have regained they become fitted to demand more. It is better that we gain what we demand by a process of negotiation which would occupy twenty years than that by communicating a sudden shock to the interests of those who are the depositories and dependents of power we should incur the calamity which their revenge might inflict upon us by giving the signal of civil war. If, after all, they consider the chance of personal ruin and the infamy of figuring on the page of history as the promoters of civil war preferable to resigning any portion how small soever of their usurped authority, we are to recollect that we possess a right beyond remonstrance. It has been acknowledged by the most approved writers on the English constitution, which is in this instance merely [a] declaration of the superior decisions of eternal justice, that we possess a right of resistance. The claim of the [reigning] family is founded upon a memorable exertion of this solemnly recorded right.

The last resort of resistance is undoubtedly insurrection. The right of insurrection is derived from the employment of armed force to counteract the will of the nation. Let the government disband the standing army, and the purpose of resistance would be sufficiently fulfilled by the incessant agitation of the points of dispute before the courts of common law and by an unwarlike display of the irresistible number and union of the people.

Before we enter into a consideration of the measures which

might terminate in civil war, let us for a moment consider the nature and the consequences of war. This is the alternative which the unprincipled cunning of the tyrants has presented to us, from which we must not sh[rink]. There is secret sympathy between destruction and power, between monarchy and war; and the long experience of the history of all recorded time teaches us with what success they have played into each other's hands. War is a kind of superstition; the pageantry of arms and badges corrupts the imagination of men. How far more appropriate would be the symbols of an inconsolable grief—muffled drums, and melancholy music, and arms reversed, and the livery of sorrow rather than of blood. When men mourn at funerals, for what do they mourn in comparison with the calamities which they hasten with all circumstance of festivity to suffer and to inflict! Visit in imagination the scene of a field of battle or a city taken by assault, collect into one group the groans and the distortions of the innumerable dying, the inconsolable grief and horror of their surviving friends, the hellish exultation, and unnatural drunkenness of destruction of the conquerors, the burning of the harvests and the obliteration of the traces of cultivation. To this, in civil war is to be added the sudden disruption of the bonds of social life, and 'father against son'.

If there had never been war, there could never have been tyranny in the world; tyrants take advantage of the mechanical organisation of armies to establish and defend their encroachments. It is thus that the mighty advantages of the French Revolution have been almost compensated by a succession of tyrants (for demagogues, oligarchies, usurpers, and legitimate kings are merely varieties of the same class) from Robespierre to Louis XVIII. War, waged from whatever motive, extinguishes the sentiment of reason and justice in the mind. The motive is forgotten, or only adverted to in a mechanical and habitual manner. A sentiment of confidence in brute force and in a contempt of death and danger is considered as the highest virtue, when in truth and however indispensable they are merely the means and the instruments, highly capable of being perverted to destroy the cause they were assumed to promote. It is a foppery the most intolerable to an amiable and philosophical mind. It is like what some reasoners have observed of religious faith; no false and indirect motive to action can subsist in the mind without weakening the effect of those which are genuine and true. The person who thinks it virtuous to believe will think a less degree of virtue attaches to good actions than if he had considered it as indifferent. The person who has been accustomed to subdue men by force will be less inclined to the trouble of convincing or persuading them.

These brief considerations suffice to show that the true friend of mankind and of his country would hesitate before he recommended measures which tend to bring down so heavy a calamity as war.

I imagine, however, that before the English nation shall arrive at that point of moral and political degradation now occupied by the Chinese, it will be necessary to appeal to an exertion of physical strength. If the madness of parties admits no other mode of determining the question at issue ...

When the people shall have obtained, by whatever means, the victory over their oppressors and when persons appointed by them shall have taken their seats in the Representative Assembly of the nation and assumed the control of public affairs according to constitutional rules, there will remain the great task of accommodating all that can be preserved of ancient forms with the improvements of the knowledge of a more enlightened age in legislation, jurisprudence, government, and religious and academical institutions. The settlement of the national debt is on the principles before elucidated merely circumstance of form, and however necessary and important is an affair of mere arithmetical proportions readily determined, nor can I see how those, who being deprived of their unjust advantages will probably inwardly murmur, can oppose one word of open expostulation to a measure of such inescapable justice.

There is one thing which certain vulgar agitators endeavour to flatter the most uneducated part of the people by assiduously proposing, which they ought not to do nor to require: and that is, Retribution. Men having been injured desire to injure in return. This is falsely called an universal law of human nature; it is a law from which many are exempt, and all in proportion to their virtue and cultivation. The savage is more revengeful than the civilised man, the ignorant and uneducated than the person of a refined and cultivated intellect; the generous and ...

[The work was left incomplete].

THE POEMS

THE MASK OF ANARCHY

Written on the occasion of the massacre at Manchester

As I lay asleep in Italy
There came a voice from over the Sea,
And with great power it forth led me
To walk in the visions of Poesy.

I met Murder on the way—
He had a mask like Castlereagh—
Very smooth he looked, yet grim;
Seven blood-hounds followed him:

All were fat; and well they might
Be in admirable plight,
For one by one, and two by two,
He tossed them human hearts to chew
Which from his wide cloak he drew.

Next came Fraud, and he had on,
Like Eldon, an ermined gown;
His big tears, for he wept well,
Turned to mill-stones as they fell.

And the little children, who
Round his feet played to and fro,
Thinking every tear a gem,
Had their brains knocked out by them.

Clothed with the Bible, as with light,
And the shadows of the night,

Like Sidmouth, next, Hypocrisy
On a crocodile rode by.

And many more Destructions played
In this ghastly masquerade,
All disguised, even to the eyes,
Like Bishops, lawyers, peers, or spies.

Last came Anarchy: he rode
On a white horse, splashed with blood;
He was pale even to the lips,
Like death in the Apocalypse.

And he wore a kingly crown;
And in his grasp a sceptre shone;
On his brow this mark I saw—
'I AM GOD, AND KING, AND LAW!'

With a pace stately and fast,
Over English land he passed,
Trampling to a mire of blood
The adoring multitude.

And a mighty troop around,
With their trampling shook the ground,
Waving each a bloody sword,
For the service of their Lord.

And with glorious triumph, they
Rode through England proud and gay,
Drunk as with intoxication
Of the wine of desolation.

O'er fields and towns, from sea to sea,
Passed the Pageant swift and free,
Tearing up, and trampling down;
Till they came to London town.

And each dweller, panic-stricken,

Felt his heart with terror sicken
Hearing the tempestuous cry
Of the triumph of Anarchy.

For with pomp to meet him came,
Clothed in arms like blood and flame,
The hired murderers, who did sing
'Thou art God, and Law, and King.

'We have waited, weak and lone
For thy coming, Mighty One!
Our purses are empty, our swords are cold,
Give us glory, and blood, and gold.'

Lawyers and priests, a motley crowd,
To the earth their pale brows bowed;
Like a bad prayer not over loud,
Whispering—'Thou art Law and God.'—

Then all cried with one accord,
'Thou art King, and God, and Lord;
Anarchy, to thee we bow,
Be thy name made holy now!'

And Anarchy, the Skeleton,
Bowed and grinned to every one,
As well as if his education,
Had cost ten millions to the nation.

For he knew the Palaces
Of our Kings were rightly his;
His the sceptre, crown, and globe,
And the gold-inwoven robe.

So he sent his slaves before
To seize upon the Bank and Tower,
And was proceeding with intent
To meet his pensioned Parliament

When one fled past, a maniac maid,
And her name was Hope, she said:
But she looked more like Despair,
And she cried out in the air:

'My father Time is weak and gray
With waiting for a better day;
See how idiot-like he stands,
Fumbling with his palsied hands!

'He has had child after child,
And the dust of death is piled
Over every one but me—
Misery, oh, Misery!'

Then she lay down in the street,
Right before the horses' feet,
Expecting, with a patient eye,
Murder, Fraud, and Anarchy.

When between her and her foes
A mist, a light, an image rose,
Small at first, and weak, and frail
Like the vapour of a vale:

Till as clouds grow on the blast,
Like tower-crowned giants striding fast,
And glare with lightnings as they fly,
And speak in thunder to the sky,

It grew—a Shape arrayed in mail
Brighter than the viper's scale,
And upborne on wings whose grain
Was as the light of sunny rain.

On its helm, seen far away,
A planet, like the Morning's, lay;
And those plumes its light rained through
Like a shower of crimson dew.

With step as soft as wind it passed
O'er the heads of men—so fast
That they knew the presence there,
And looked,—but all was empty air.

As flowers beneath May's footstep waken,
As stars from Night's loose hair are shaken,
As waves arise when loud winds call,
Thoughts sprung where'er that step did fall.

And the prostrate multitude
Looked—and ankle-deep in blood,
Hope, that maiden most serene,
Was walking with a quiet mien:

And Anarchy, the ghastly birth,
Lay dead earth upon the earth;
The Horse of Death tameless as wind
Fled, and with his hoofs did grind
To dust the murderers thronged behind.

A rushing light of clouds and splendour,
A sense awakening and yet tender
Was heard and felt—and at its close
These words of joy and fear arose

As if their own indignant Earth
Which gave the sons of England birth
Had felt their blood upon her brow,
And shuddering with a mother's throe

Had turned every drop of blood
By which her face had been bedewed
To an accent unwithstood,—
As if her heart had cried aloud:

'Men of England, heirs of Glory,
Heroes of unwritten story,

Nurslings of one mighty Mother,
Hopes of her, and one another;

'Rise like Lions after slumber
In unvanquishable number,
Shake your chains to earth like dew
Which in sleep had fallen on you—
Ye are many—they are few.

'What is Freedom?—ye can tell
That which slavery is, too well—
For its very name has grown
To an echo of your own.

''Tis to work and have such pay
As just keeps life from day to day
In your limbs, as in a cell
For the tyrants' use to dwell,

'So that ye for them are made
Loom, and plough, and sword, and spade,
With or without your own will bent
To their defence and nourishment.

''Tis to see your children weak
With their mothers pine and peak,
When the winter winds are bleak,—
They are dying whilst I speak.

''Tis to hunger for such diet
As the rich man in his riot
Casts to the fat dogs that lie
Surfeiting beneath his eye;

''Tis to let the Ghost of Gold
Take from Toil a thousandfold
More than e'er its substance could
In the tyrannies of old.

'Paper coin—that forgery
Of the title-deeds, which ye
Hold to something of the worth
Of the inheritance of Earth.

''Tis to be a slave in soul
And to hold no strong control
Over your own wills, but be
All that others make of ye.

'And at length when ye complain
With a murmur weak and vain
'Tis to see the Tyrant's crew
Ride over your wives and you—
Blood is on the grass like dew.

'Then it is to feel revenge
Fiercely thirsting to exchange
Blood for blood—and wrong for wrong—
Do not thus when ye are strong.

'Birds find rest, in narrow nest
When weary of their winged quest;
Beasts find fare, in woody lair
When storm and snow are in the air.

'Asses, swine, have litter spread
And with fitting food are fed;
All things have a home but one—
Thou, oh Englishman, hast none!

'This is slavery—savage men,
Or wild beasts within a den
Would endure not as ye do—
But such ills they never knew.

'What art thou Freedom? O! could slaves
Answer from their living graves

This demand—tyrants would flee
Like a dream's dim imagery:

'Thou art not, as impostors say,
A shadow soon to pass away,
A superstition, and a name
Echoing from the cave of Fame.

'For the labourer thou art bread,
And a comely table spread
From his daily labour come
In a neat and happy home.

'Thou art clothes, and fire, and food
For the trampled multitude—
No—in countries that are free
Such starvation cannot be
As in England now we see.

'To the rich thou art a check,
When his foot is on the neck
Of his victim, thou dost make
That he treads upon a snake.

'Thou art Justice—ne'er for gold
May thy righteous laws be sold
As laws are in England—thou
Shield'st alike the high and low.

'Thou art Wisdom—Freemen never
Dream that God will damn for ever
All who think those things untrue
Of which Priests make such ado.

'Thou art Peace—never by thee
Would blood and treasure wasted be
As tyrants wasted them, when all
Leagued to quench thy flame in Gaul.

'What if English toil and blood
Was poured forth, even as a flood?
It availed, Oh, Liberty,
To dim, but not extinguish thee.

'Thou art Love—the rich have kissed
Thy feet, and like him following Christ,
Give their substance to the free
And through the rough world follow thee,

'Or turn their wealth to arms, and make
War for thy beloved sake
On wealth, and war, and fraud—whence they
Drew the power which is their prey.

'Science, Poetry, and Thought
Are thy lamps; they make the lot
Of the dwellers in a cot
So serene, they curse it not.

'Spirit, Patience, Gentleness,
All that can adorn and bless
Art thou—let deeds, not words, express
Thine exceeding loveliness.

'Let a great Assembly be
Of the fearless and the free
On some spot of English ground
Where the plains stretch wide around.

'Let the blue sky overhead,
The green earth on which ye tread,
All that must eternal be
Witness the solemnity.

'From the corners uttermost
Of the bounds of English coast;
From every hut, village, and town

Where those who live and suffer moan
For others' misery or their own.

'From the workhouse and the prison
Where pale as corpses newly risen,
Women, children, young and old
Groan for pain, and weep for cold—

'From the haunts of daily life
Where is waged the daily strife
With common wants and common cares
Which sows the human heart with tares—

'Lastly from the palaces
Where the murmur of distress
Echoes, like the distant sound
Of a wind alive around

'Those prison halls of wealth and fashion,
Where some few feel such compassion
For those who groan. and toil, and wail
As must make their brethren pale—

'Ye who suffer woes untold,
Or to feel, or to behold
Your lost country bought and sold
With a price of blood and gold—

'Let a vast assembly be,
And with great solemnity
Declare with measured words that ye
Are, as God has made ye, free—

'Be your strong and simple words
Keen to wound as sharpened swords,
And wide as targes let them be,
With their shade to cover ye.

'Let the tyrants pour around

With a quick and startling sound,
Like the loosening of a sea,
Troops of armed emblazonry.

'Let the charged artillery drive
Till the dead air seems alive
With the clash of clanging wheels
And the tramp of horses' heels.

'Let the fixed bayonet
Gleam with sharp desire to wet
Its bright point in English blood
Looking keen as one for food.

'Let the horsemen's scimitars
Wheel and flash, like sphereless stars
Thirsting to eclipse their burning
In a sea of death and mourning.

'Stand ye calm and resolute,
Like a forest close and mute,
With folded arms and looks which are
Weapons of unvanquished war.

'And let Panic, who outspeeds
The career of armed steeds
Pass, a disregarded shade
Through your phalanx undismayed.

'Let the laws of your own land,
Good or ill, between ye stand
Hand to hand, and foot to foot,
Arbiters of the dispute,

'The old laws of England—they
Whose reverend heads with age are gray,
Children of a wiser day;
And whose solemn voice must be
Thine own echo—Liberty!

'On those who first should violate
Such sacred heralds in their state
Rest the blood that must ensue,
And it will not rest on you.

'And if then the tyrants dare
Let them ride among you there,
Slash, and stab, and maim, and hew,—
What they like, that let them do.

'With folded arms and steady eyes,
And little fear, and less surprise,
Look upon them as they slay
Till their rage has died away.

'Then they will return with shame
To the place from which they came,
And the blood thus shed will speak
In hot blushes on their cheek.

'Every woman in the land
Will point at them as they stand—
They will hardly dare to greet
Their acquaintance in the street.

'And the bold, true warriors
Who have hugged Danger in wars
Will turn to those who would be free,
Ashamed of such base company.

'And that slaughter to the Nation
Shall steam up like inspiration,
Eloquent, oracular;
A volcano heard afar.

'And these words shall then become
Like Oppression's thundered doom
Ringing through each heart and brain,
Heard again—again—again—

'Rise like Lions after slumber
In unvanquishable number—
Shake your chains to earth like dew
Which in sleep had fallen on you—
Ye are many—they are few.'

LINES WRITTEN DURING THE CASTLEREAGH ADMINISTRATION

Corpses are cold in the tomb;
Stones on the pavement are dumb;
Abortions are dead in the womb,
And their mothers look pale—like the death-white shore
Of Albion, free no more.

Her sons are as stones in the way—
They are masses of senseless clay—
They are trodden and move not away,—
The abortion with which *she* travaileth
Is Liberty, smitten to death.

Then trample and dance, thou Oppressor!
For thy victim is no redresser;
Thou art sole lord and possessor
Of her corpses, and clods, and abortions—they pave
Thy path to the grave.

Hearest thou the festival din
Of Death, and Destruction, and Sin,
And Wealth crying *Havoc!* within?
'Tis the bacchanal triumph that makes Truth dumb,
Thine Epithalamium.

Ay, marry thy ghastly wife!
Let Fear and Disquiet and Strife
Spread thy couch in the chamber of Life!
Marry Ruin, thou Tyrant! and Hell be thy guide
To the bed of the bride!

SONG TO THE MEN OF ENGLAND

Men of England, wherefore plough
For the lords who lay ye low?
Wherefore weave with toil and care
The rich robes your tyrants wear?

Wherefore feed, and clothe, and save,
From the cradle to the grave,
Those ungrateful drones who would
Drain your sweat—nay, drink your blood?

Wherefore, Bees of England, forge
Many a weapon, chain, and scourge,
That these stingless drones may spoil
The forced produce of your toil?

Have ye leisure, comfort, calm,
Shelter, food, love's gentle balm?
Or what is it ye buy so dear
With your pain and with your fear?

The seed ye sow, another reaps;
The wealth ye find, another keeps;
The robes ye weave, another wears;
The arms ye forge, another bears.

Sow seed,—but let no tyrant reap;
Find wealth,—let no impostor heap;
Weave robes,—let not the idle wear;
Forge arms,—in your defence to bear.

Shrink to your cellars, holes, and cells;
In halls ye deck another dwells.
Why shake the chains ye wrought? Ye see
The steel ye tempered glance on ye.

With plough and spade, and hoe and loom,
Trace your grave, and build your tomb,
And weave your winding-sheet, till fair
England be your sepulchre.

SIMILES FOR TWO POLITICAL CHARACTERS OF 1819

As from an ancestral oak
Two empty ravens sound their clarion,
Yell by yell, and croak by croak,
When they scent the noonday smoke
Of fresh human carrion:—

As two gibbering night-birds flit
From their bowers of deadly yew
Through the night to frighten it,
When the moon is in a fit,
And the stars are none, or few:—

As a shark and dog-fish wait
Under an Atlantic isle,
For the negro-ship, whose freight
Is the theme of their debate,
Wrinkling their red gills the while—

Are ye, two vultures sick for battle,
Two scorpions under one wet stone,
Two bloodless wolves whose dry throats rattle,
Two crows perched on the murrained cattle,
Two vipers tangled into one.

'WHAT MEN GAIN FAIRLY'

What men gain fairly—that they should possess,
And children may inherit idleness,
From him who earns it—This is understood;
Private injustice may be general good.
But he who gains by base and armed wrong,
Or guilty fraud, or base compliances,
May be despoiled; even as a stolen dress
Is stripped from a convicted thief, and he
Left in the nakedness of infamy.

A NEW NATIONAL ANTHEM

God prosper, speed and save,
God raise from England's grave
Her murdered Queen!
Pave with swift victory
The steps of Liberty,
Whom Britons own to be
Immortal Queen.

See, she comes throned on high,
On swift Eternity!
God save the Queen!
Millions on millions wait,
Firm, rapid, and elate,
On her majestic state!
God save the Queen!

She is Thine own pure soul
Moulding the mighty whole,—
God save the Queen!
She is Thine own deep love
Rained down from Heaven above,—
Wherever she rest or move,
God save our Queen!

'Wilder her enemies
In their own dark disguise,—
God save our Queen!
All earthly things that dare
Her sacred name to bear,

Strip them, as kings are, bare;
God save the Queen!

Be her eternal throne
Built in our hearts alone—
God save the Queen!
Let the oppressor hold
Canopied seats of gold;
She sits enthroned of old
O'er our hearts Queen.

Lips touched by seraphim
Breathe out the choral hymn
'God save the Queen!'
Sweet as if angels sang,
Loud as that trumpet's clang
Wakening the world's dead gang,—
God save the Queen!

SONNET: ENGLAND IN 1819

An old, mad, blind, despised, and dying king,—
Princes, the dregs of their dull race, who flow
Through public scorn,—mud from a muddy spring,—
Rulers who neither see, nor feel, nor know,
But leech-like to their fainting country cling,
Till they drop, blind in blood, without a blow,—
A people starved and stabbed in the untilled field,—
An army, which liberticide and prey
Makes as a two-edged sword to all who wield,—
Golden and sanguine laws which tempt and slay;
Religion Christless, Godless—a book sealed;
A Senate,—Time's worst statute unrepealed,—
Are graves, from which a glorious Phantom may
Burst, to illumine our tempestuous day.

BALLAD OF THE STARVING MOTHER

Young Parson Richards stood at his gate
Feeding his hound with bread;
Hunch after hunch the mere beast ate,
Moving his tail and his head.

A woman came up with a babe at her breast
Which was flaccid with toil and hunger;
She cried: 'Give me food and give me rest—
We die if we wait much longer.

'The poor thing sucks and no milk will come,
He would cry but his strength is gone,—
His wasting weakness has left him dumb,
Ye can hardly hear him moan.

'The skin around his eyes is pale and blue,
His eyes are glazed, not with tears—
I wish for a little moment that you
Could know what a mother fears.

'Give me a piece of that fine white bread—
I would give you some blood for it—
Before I faint and my infant is dead!
O give me a little bit!

'Alas, it was sold, that trinket of gold
Which my ruiner gave to me;
All the winter nights on my bosom, as cold
It lay, as his heart might be.

'And the single blanket of threadbare woof,
Under which we both cried to sleep,
Is gone—the rain drenches us through the roof—
And I moan, but no longer weep.

'What would it avail me to prostitute
This lean body, squalid and wild?
And yet by the God who made me I'd do't
If I could but save my child!

'Perhaps you would like—but, alas, you are
A staid and a holy man—
And, if you were not, . . . would any one care
For these limbs so meagre and wan?

'Aye, aye, one as rich and as grave as you
Once found them a dear delight;
I scarce think he would be as cruel now
If he saw them in this sad plight.

'Give me bread—my hot bowels gnaw—
I'll tear down the garden gate—
I'll fight with the dog,—I'll tear from his maw
The crust which he just has ate—

'Priest, consider that God who created us
Meant this for a world of love—
Remember the story of Lazarus,
You preach to the people of—

'And, upon my soul, I begin to think
'Twere a joy beyond all pleasure
To sit up in Heaven, and see you drink
In Hell, of your own true measure.

'Will you say God said this to frighten the rich?
He will only damn the poor?
That the deadly sins are above those which
There are many temptations for?

'We doubt, the great Power has made us each
Such as we were to be . . .
And then to damn us, the thing would impeach
His justice and charity!

'And yet I cannot imagine how we
Can call him just and good,
When he sends a wretched woman like me
To a man like you for food.

'O God! this poor dear child did I
At thy command bear and cherish!
Thou bads't us increase and multiply—
And our tyrants bid us perish!

'Water! Water! and bread and beer!
A little morsel of bread!—
My own dear baby is dying I fear!—
And I—I hope—am dead.'

The man of God with a surly frown
To the garden wicket paced,
And he saw the woman had fallen down
With her face below her waist.

The child lay stiff as a frozen straw
In the woman's white cold breast—
And the parson in its dead features saw
His own to the truth expressed!

He turned from the bosom whose heart was broke—
Once it pillowed him as he slept—
He turned from the lips that no longer spoke,
From the eyes that no longer wept.

ODE TO LIBERTY

Yet, Freedom, yet, thy banner, torn but flying,
Streams like a thunder-storm against the wind.
—BYRON

A glorious people vibrated again
The lightning of the nations: Liberty
From heart to heart, from tower to tower, o'er Spain,
Scattering contagious fire into the sky,
Gleamed. My soul spurned the chains of its dismay,
And in the rapid plumes of song
Clothed itself, sublime and strong,
(As a young eagle soars the morning clouds among,)
Hovering in verse o'er its accustomed prey;
Till from its station in the Heaven of fame
The spirit's whirlwind rapped it, and the ray
Of the remotest sphere of living flame
Which paves the void was from behind it flung,
As foam from a ship's swiftness, when there came
A voice out of the deep: I will record the same.

The Sun and the serenest Moon sprang forth:
The burning stars of the abyss were hurled
Into the depths of Heaven. The daedal earth,
That island in the ocean of the world,
Hung in its cloud of all-sustaining air:
But this divinest universe
Was yet a chaos and a curse,
For thou wert not: but, power from worst producing worse,

The spirit of the beasts was kindled there,
And of the birds, and of the watery forms,
And there was war among them, and despair
Within them, raging without truce or terms:
The bosom of their violated nurse
Groaned, for beasts warred on beasts, and worms on worms,
And men on men; each heart was as a hell of storms.

Man, the imperial shape, then multiplied
His generations under the pavilion
Of the Sun's throne: palace and pyramid,
Temple and prison, to many a swarming million
Were, as to mountain-wolves their ragged caves.
This human living multitude
Was savage, cunning, blind, and rude,
For thou wert not; but o'er the populous solitude,
Like one fierce cloud over a waste of waves,
Hung Tyranny; beneath, sate deified
The sister-pest, congregator of slaves;
Into the shadow of her pinions wide
Anarchs and priests, who feed on gold and blood
Till with the stain their inmost souls are dyed,
Drove the astonished herds of men from every side.

The nodding promontories, and blue isles,
And cloud-like mountains, and dividuous waves
Of Greece, basked glorious in the open smiles
Of favouring Heaven: from their enchanted caves
Prophetic echoes flung dim melody.
On the unapprehensive wild
The vine, the corn, the olive mild,
Grew savage yet, to human use unreconciled;
And, like unfolded flowers beneath the sea,
Like the man's thought dark in the infant's brain,
Like aught that is which wraps what is to be,
Art's deathless dreams lay veiled by many a vein

Of Parian stone; and, yet a speechless child,
Verse murmured, and Philosophy did strain
Her lidless eyes for thee; when o'er the Aegean main

Athens arose: a city such as vision
Builds from the purple crags and silver towers
Of battlemented cloud, as in derision
Of kingliest masonry: the ocean-floors
Pave it; the evening sky pavilions it;
Its portals are inhabited
By thunder-zoned winds, each head
Within its cloudy wings with sun-fire garlanded,—
A divine work! Athens, diviner yet,
Gleamed with its crest of columns, on the will
Of man, as a mount of diamond, set;
For thou wert, and thine all-creative skill
Peopled, with forms that mock the eternal dead
In marble immortality, that hill
Which was thine earliest throne and latest oracle.

Within the surface of Time's fleeting river
Its wrinkled image lies, as then it lay
Immovably unquiet, and for ever
It trembles, but it cannot pass away!
The voices of thy bards and sages thunder
With an earth-awakening blast
Through the caverns of the past:
(Religion veils her eyes; Oppression shrinks aghast:)
A winged sound of joy, and love, and wonder,
Which soars where Expectation never flew,
Rending the veil of space and time asunder!
One ocean feeds the clouds, and streams, and dew;
One Sun illumines Heaven; one Spirit vast
With life and love makes chaos ever new,
As Athens doth the world with thy delight renew.

Then Rome was, and from thy deep bosom fairest,
Like a wolf-cub from a Cadmaean Maenad,
She drew the milk of greatness, though thy dearest
From that Elysian food was yet unweaned;
And many a deed of terrible uprightness
By thy sweet love was sanctified;
And in thy smile, and by thy side,
Saintly Camillus lived, and firm Atilius died.
But when tears stained thy robe of vestal whiteness,
And gold profaned thy Capitolian throne,
Thou didst desert, with spirit-winged lightness,
The senate of the tyrants: they sunk prone
Slaves of one tyrant: Palatinus sighed
Faint echoes of Ionian song; that tone
Thou didst delay to hear, lamenting to disown.

From what Hyrcanian glen or frozen hill,
Or piny promontory of the Arctic main,
Or utmost islet inaccessible,
Didst thou lament the ruin of thy reign,
Teaching the woods and waves, and desert rocks,
And every Naiad's ice-cold urn,
To talk in echoes sad and stern
Of that sublimest lore which man had dared unlearn?
For neither did thou watch the wizard flocks
Of the Scald's dreams, nor haunt the Druid's sleep.
What if the tears rained through thy shattered locks
Were quickly dried? for thou didst groan, not weep,
When from its sea of death, to kill and burn,
The Galilean serpent forth did creep,
And made thy world an undistinguishable heap.

A thousand years the Earth cried, 'Where art thou?'
And then the shadow of thy coming fell
On Saxon Alfred's olive-cinctured brow:
And many a warrior-peopled citadel.

Like rocks which fire lifts out of the flat deep,
Arose in sacred Italy,
Frowning o'er the tempestuous sea
Of kings, and priests, and slaves, in tower-crowned majesty;
That multitudinous anarchy did sweep
And burst around their walls, like idle foam,
Whilst from the human spirit's deepest deep
Strange melody with love and awe struck dumb
Dissonant arms; and Art, which cannot die,
With divine wand traced on our earthly home
Fit imagery to pave Heaven's everlasting dome.

Thou huntress swifter than the Moon! thou terror
Of the world's wolves! thou bearer of the quiver,
Whose sunlike shafts pierce tempest-winged Error,
As light may pierce the clouds when they dissever
In the calm regions of the orient day!
Luther caught thy wakening glance;
Like lightning, from his leaden lance
Reflected, it dissolved the visions of the trance
In which, as in a tomb, the nations lay;
And England's prophets hailed thee as their queen,
In songs whose music cannot pass away,
Though it must flow forever: not unseen
Before the spirit-sighted countenance
Of Milton didst thou pass, from the sad scene
Beyond whose night he saw, with a dejected mien.

The eager hours and unreluctant years
As on a dawn-illumined mountain stood,
Trampling to silence their loud hopes and fears,
Darkening each other with their multitude,
And cried aloud, 'Liberty!' Indignation
Answered Pity from her cave;
Death grew pale within the grave,
And Desolation howled to the destroyer, Save!

When like Heaven's Sun girt by the exhalation
Of its own glorious light, thou didst arise,
Chasing thy foes from nation unto nation
Like shadows: as if day had cloven the skies
At dreaming midnight o'er the western wave,
Men started, staggering with a glad surprise,
Under the lightnings of thine unfamiliar eyes.

Thou Heaven of earth! what spells could pall thee then
In ominous eclipse? a thousand years
Bred from the slime of deep Oppression's den,
Dyed all thy liquid light with blood and tears,
Till thy sweet stars could weep the stain away;
How like Bacchanals of blood
Round France, the ghastly vintage, stood
Destruction's sceptred slaves, and Folly's mitred brood!
When one, like them, but mightier far than they,
The Anarch of thine own bewildered powers,
Rose: armies mingled in obscure array,
Like clouds with clouds, darkening the sacred bowers
Of serene Heaven. He, by the past pursued,
Rests with those dead, but unforgotten hours,
Whose ghosts scare victor kings in their ancestral towers.

England yet sleeps: was she not called of old?
Spain calls her now, as with its thrilling thunder
Vesuvius awakens Aetna, and the cold
Snow-crags by its reply are cloven in sunder:
O'er the lit waves every Aeolian isle
From Pithecusa to Pelorus
Howls, and leaps, and glares in chorus:
They cry, 'Be dim; ye lamps of Heaven suspended o'er us!'
Her chains are threads of gold, she need but smile
And they dissolve; but Spain's were links of steel,
Till bit to dust by virtue's keenest file.
Twins of a single destiny! appeal

To the eternal years enthroned before us
In the dim West; impress us from a seal,
All ye have thought and done! Time cannot dare conceal.

Tomb of Arminius! render up thy dead
Till, like a standard from a watch-tower's staff,
His soul may stream over the tyrant's head;
Thy victory shall be his epitaph,
Wild Bacchanal of truth's mysterious wine,
King-deluded Germany,
His dead spirit lives in thee.
Why do we fear or hope? thou art already free!
And thou, lost Paradise of this divine
And glorious world! thou flowery wilderness!
Thou island of eternity! thou shrine
Where Desolation, clothed with loveliness,
Worships the thing thou wert! O Italy,
Gather thy blood into thy heart; repress
The beasts who make their dens thy sacred palaces.

Oh, that the free would stamp the impious name
Of KING into the dust! or write it there,
So that this blot upon the page of fame
Were as a serpent's path, which the light air
Erases, and the flat sands close behind!
Ye the oracle have heard:
Lift the victory-flashing sword,
And cut the snaky knots of this foul gordian word,
Which, weak itself as stubble, yet can bind
Into a mass, irrefragably firm,
The axes and the rods which awe mankind;
The sound has poison in it, 'tis the sperm
Of what makes life foul, cankerous, and abhorred;
Disdain not thou, at thine appointed term,
To set thine armed heel on this reluctant worm.

Oh, that the wise from their bright minds would kindle
Such lamps within the dome of this dim world,
That the pale name of PRIEST might shrink and dwindle
Into the hell from which it first was hurled,
A scoff of impious pride from fiends impure;
Till human thoughts might kneel alone,
Each before the judgement-throne
Of its own aweless soul, or of the Power unknown!
Oh, that the words which make the thoughts obscure
From which they spring, as clouds of glimmering dew
From a white lake blot Heaven's blue portraiture,
Were stripped of their thin masks and various hue
And frowns and smiles and splendours not their own,
Till in the nakedness of false and true
They stand before their Lord, each to receive its due!

He who taught man to vanquish whatsoever
Can be between the cradle and the grave
Crowned him the King of Life. Oh, vain endeavour!
If on his own high will, a willing slave,
He has enthroned the oppression and the oppressor.
What if earth can clothe and feed
Amplest millions at their need,
And power in thought be as the tree within the seed?
Or what if Art, an ardent intercessor,
Driving on fiery wings to Nature's throne,
Checks the great mother stooping to caress her,
And cries, 'Give me, thy child, dominion
Over all height and depth'? if Life can breed
New wants, and wealth from those who toil and groan,
Rend of thy gifts and hers a thousandfold for one!

Come thou, but lead out of the inmost cave
Of man's deep spirit, as the morning-star
Beckons the Sun from the Eoan wave,
Wisdom. I hear the pennons of her car

Self-moving, like cloud charioted by flame;
Comes she not, and come ye not,
Rulers of eternal thought,
To judge, with solemn truth, life's ill-apportioned lot?
Blind Love, and equal Justice, and the Fame
Of what has been, the Hope of what will be?
O Liberty! if such could be thy name
Wert thou disjoined from these, or they from thee:
If thine or theirs were treasures to be bought
By blood or tears, have not the wise and free
Wept tears, and blood like tears?—The solemn harmony

Paused, and the spirit of that mighty singing
To its abyss was suddenly withdrawn;
Then, as a wild swan, when sublimely winging
Its path athwart the thunder-smoke of dawn,
Sinks headlong through the aereal golden light
On the heavy-sounding plain,
When the bolt has pierced its brain;
As summer clouds dissolve, unburthened of their rain;
As a far taper fades with fading night,
As a brief insect dies with dying day,—
My song, its pinions disarrayed of might,
Drooped; o'er it closed the echoes far away
Of the great voice which did its flight sustain,
As waves which lately paved his watery way
Hiss round a drowner's head in their tempestuous play.

ODE TO THE WEST WIND

O wild West Wind, thou breath of Autumn's being,
Thou, from whose unseen presence the leaves dead
Are driven, like ghosts from an enchanter fleeing,

Yellow, and black, and pale, and hectic red,
Pestilence-stricken multitudes: O thou,
Who chariotest to their dark wintry bed

The winged seeds, where they lie cold and low,
Each like a corpse within its grave, until
Thine azure sister of the Spring shall blow

Her clarion o'er the dreaming earth, and fill
(Driving sweet buds like flocks to feed in air)
With living hues and odours plain and hill:

Wild Spirit, which art moving everywhere;
Destroyer and preserver; hear, oh, hear!

Thou on whose stream, mid the steep sky's commotion,
Loose clouds like earth's decaying leaves are shed,
Shook from the tangled boughs of Heaven and Ocean,

Angels of rain and lightning: there are spread
On the blue surface of thine aery surge,
Like the bright hair uplifted from the head

Of some fierce Maenad, even from the dim verge
Of the horizon to the zenith's height,
The locks of the approaching storm. Thou dirge

Of the dying year, to which this closing night
Will be the dome of a vast sepulchre,
Vaulted with all thy congregated might

Of vapours, from whose solid atmosphere
Black rain, and fire, and hail will burst: oh, hear!

Thou who didst waken from his summer dreams
The blue Mediterranean, where he lay,
Lulled by the coil of his crystalline streams,

Beside a pumice isle in Baiae's bay,
And saw in sleep old palaces and towers
Quivering within the wave's intenser day,

All overgrown with azure moss and flowers
So sweet, the sense faints picturing them! Thou
For whose path the Atlantic's level powers

Cleave themselves into chasms, while far below
The sea-blooms and the oozy woods which wear
The sapless foliage of the ocean, know

Thy voice, and suddenly grow gray with fear,
And tremble and despoil themselves: oh, hear!

If I were a dead leaf thou mightest bear;
If I were a swift cloud to fly with thee;
A wave to pant beneath thy power, and share

The impulse of thy strength, only less free
Than thou, O uncontrollable! If even
I were as in my boyhood, and could be

The comrade of thy wanderings over Heaven,
As then, when to outstrip thy skiey speed
Scarce seemed a vision; I would ne'er have striven

As thus with thee in prayer in my sore need.
Oh, lift me as a wave, a leaf, a cloud!

I fall upon the thorns of life! I bleed!

A heavy weight of hours has chained and bowed
One too like thee: tameless, and swift, and proud.

Make me thy lyre, even as the forest is:
What if my leaves are falling like its own!
The tumult of thy mighty harmonies

Will take from both a deep, autumnal tone,
Sweet though in sadness. Be thou, Spirit fierce,
My spirit! Be thou me, impetuous one!

Drive my dead thoughts over the universe
Like withered leaves to quicken a new birth!
And, by the incantation of this verse,

Scatter, as from an unextinguished hearth
Ashes and sparks, my words among mankind!
Be through my lips to unawakened earth

The trumpet of a prophecy! O, Wind,
If Winter comes, can Spring be far behind?

Paul Foot

Red Shelley

The poet Shelley was an outcast in his own lifetime:
an atheist whose poetry attacked the bigotry of the church;
a socialist who castigated the viciously repressive Tory
government of the time; a republican who took up the
cause of Irish freedom; a supporter of women's rights
years ahead of his time. For these views he was forced out
of England into exile. For years the literary establishment
censored Shelley's views to portray a romantic with his
head in the clouds. This book sets the record straight.
288 pages paperback

£4.95

From bookshops, or by post (add 60p postage) from
BOOKMARKS, 265 Seven Sisters Road, Finsbury
Park, London N4 2DE.